INSIGHTS F
LIFE BETWE

EXPLORING THE
ETERNAL
SOUL

First published by O Books, 2007
O Books is an imprint of John Hunt Publishing Ltd.,
The Bothy, Deershot Lodge, Park Lane, Ropley, Hants, SO24 0BE, UK
office1@o-books.net
www.o-books.net

Distribution in:

UK and Europe
Orca Book Services
orders@orcabookservices.co.uk
Tel: 01202 665432 Fax: 01202 666219 Int. code (44)

USA and Canada
NBN
custserv@nbnbooks.com
Tel: 1 800 462 6420 Fax: 1 800 338 4550

Australia and New Zealand
Brumby Books
sales@brumbybooks.com.au
Tel: 61 3 9761 5535 Fax: 61 3 9761 7095

Far East (offices in Singapore, Thailand, Hong Kong, Taiwan)
Pansing Distribution Pte Ltd
kemal@pansing.com
Tel: 65 6319 9939 Fax: 65 6462 5761

South Africa
Alternative Books
altbook@peterhyde.co.za
Tel: 021 447 5300 Fax: 021 447 1430

Text copyright Andy Tomlinson 2007

Design: Stuart Davies

ISBN: 978 1 84694 069 9

A CIP catalogue record for this book is available from the British Library.

Printed in the US by Maple Vail

To contact Andy Tomlinson or find out more about his work visit the website
http://www.regressionacademy.com.

INSIGHTS FROM THE
LIFE BETWEEN LIVES

EXPLORING THE
ETERNAL
SOUL

ANDY TOMLINSON

BOOKS

Winchester, UK
Washington, USA

CONTENTS

PREFACE   **1**

INTRODUCTION   **3**
Laying the foundations; the reliability of interlife material;
the mechanics of interlife regression; progressing interlife
research; the presentation of transcripts.

1. TOWARDS THE LIGHT   **11**
The three realms; leaving the body; welcoming parties;
the tunnel.

2. BECOMING WHOLE AGAIN   **27**
Healing; delayering; dealing with trauma; special rest;
reintegrating soul energy.

3. REVIEWING PAST LIVES   **49**
Soul perspective; solitary reflections; spirit guide reviews;
the library of life books; reviews with the elders.

4. SOUL GROUPS   **73**
Soul mates; soul experience; group dynamics;spirit guides.

5. SPECIALIST ACTIVITIES   **85**
Healers, guides and teachers; intellectual pursuits; working
with energy.

6. PLANNING THE NEXT LIFE   **97**
Planning with other souls; single life previews; multiple
choice previews; planning with the elders; recaps, reminders
and triggers.

7. KARMIC DYNAMICS   **127**
Learning, experience and growth; the role of freewill;
emotional lessons and specialist skills; altruistic lives.

8. RETURNING TO INCARNATION   **135**
Selecting energies, emotions and strengths;
embarkation and relayering; merging with the body;
the veil of amnesia.

9. CONCLUSION   **153**
Guidance and support; subject feedback; final thoughts.

APPENDIX   **161**
The history of interlife; research details; questions used for the
subject feedback; comparion with other interlife pioneers.

GLOSSARY   **169**

SOURCE REFERENCES   **173**

BIBLIOGRAPHY   **177**

INDEX   **179**

ABOUT THE AUTHOR   **181**

FURTHER READING   **183**

PREFACE

I have been a past life and regression therapist for over ten years and have helped hundreds of clients to overcome various psychological problems, including allowing them a glimpse of death following a past life. In 2003 I came across the work of other past life pioneers who had regressed people beyond a past life and into the interlife. This was my inspiration to start on the path of becoming an interlife regression therapist myself. In 2006 my first book *Healing the Eternal Soul* was published which included a chapter on interlife regression. As I was writing it I knew that this was an area I wanted to expand into a full book. I mentioned this to a close colleague Ian Lawton who had just completed writing a book called the *Book of the Soul*. We had the idea of working together. Ian would add his analytic and research ability, and I would add my interlife knowledge and skills. Following our joint research it became clear that the information was best suited to become two books to appeal to somewhat different audiences.

This is the first book from the research and covers the individual experience of ordinary people who have had an interlife regression. It explores the incredible world that awaits us all following physical death. New and exciting information from the interlife is identified as this territory is further explored and charted. Ian assisted by producing the analysis of the transcripts and the book outline, and I need to thank him for his amazing skills. The research went further by asking structured questions on a wide range of subjects to the evolved spirits of light encountered during the interlife. New techniques were developed to tap into incredible knowledge, and Ian has written this part into a companion book called the *Wisdom of the Soul*.

I would like to thank the subjects for giving their time generously and in providing feedback afterwards. They showed a good deal of courage and selflessness in sharing their personal interlife experiences with the world. I would like to express my sincerest gratitude to all of them. This also extends to Liz Swanson for the arduous task of transcribing the regression session tapes.

If this book inspires its readers to explore their own interlife then a list of professionally trained therapists can be found on my website; *www.regressionacademy.com.*

INTRODUCTION

I want to know what sustains you from the inside
when all else falls away.
I want to know if you can be alone with yourself,
and if you like the company you keep in the empty moments.
Mountain Dreamer, Oriah Indian Elder.

Laying the Foundation

The idea that we have past lives is becoming more widespread and an increasing number of people are having their own experience. The therapists who offer past life regression frequently use hypnotic trance. This enables past life memories to quickly surface into conscious awareness, and often with amazing clarity.

Skeptics say that past-life memories are simply the product of the human imagination to construct a plausible story. The necessary information may have been obtained by perfectly normal means over the course of the person's lifetime. They may also point out factual inaccuracies. However this is too slight a dismissal of such a complex phenomenon.

There are a number of reasons to take past-life memories seriously. First, a considerable number of independently investigated cases have been published in which people have recalled information that has been subsequently verified. Often this information is obscure and so detailed about the period of the past life that it is unlikely to have been obtained by normal means. Also the circumstances of many of these cases have been fully investigated without any signs of deliberate deception.

Another reason is the professionalism of past-life therapists. Some skeptics suggest that the therapists are unprofessional and give leading suggestions to clients because they believe in reincarnation themselves. This is a long way from the truth. Many pioneers in the sixties and early seventies were professionally trained psychologists and psychiatrists. The Americans include Michael Newton, Morris Netherton, Edith Fiore, Helen Wambach and Brian Weiss. The others include British Roger Woolger, Canadian Joel Whitton, Australian Peter Ramster and Dutchman Hans TenDam. Nearly all of them described how they had become atheists while studying at university. Using conventional hypnosis to regress their clients back into childhood they experimentally stumbled upon what appeared to be past lives. Without exception they came to believe in their authenticity because of the incredible therapeutic effects produced by their recall. Some clients who had failed to respond to conventional therapies over many years made dramatic improvements after only a few sessions.

Skeptics may suggest that people only remember past lives of being famous and this is because of their ego. However, this is incorrect because many past lives are as ordinary people in the cultural conditions that have prevailed throughout human history. In some cases the past lives are nasty, brutal and short. Importantly all the past lives are significant to the person experiencing it. Often they report a full range of emotions including fear, anger and sadness as the past-life is reported. This strongly contradicts any suggestion that these are mere fantasies.

The final area that needs to be examined is the research into children who spontaneously remember past lives. Professor Ian Stevenson and his team at the University of Virginia have investigated and documented thousands of cases in which the children's reports of past lives have been subsequently verified. Often the information was so obscure it could not be explained away except through reincarnation. For example, one five-year old child reported 49 specific details of a past-life experience that was later verified by at least two independent witnesses who knew the past-life person. This research together with all the other evidence provides a compelling case that past lives are to be taken seriously.

The Reliability of Interlife Information

The obvious question is what happens between lives? In an interlife regression clients report there is a transition to the light following a past life death. The descriptions are often of looking back at the scene below or quickly moving to the light. If the past life death has been traumatic such as from a battle, execution or accident, many of these harsh memories are still present. Healing and rest is offered in the afterlife. At some point a review of the past life takes place, often with a spirit guide. This is an evolved soul that has been overseeing the past life.

At a later point the narrative moves to meeting a soul group. These are souls that work together and often jointly reincarnate on some meaningful work. The highlight during an interlife is to meet the 'elders' who are souls who have attained a level of experience and wisdom that not does require them to physically reincarnate. They review the progress of the soul before them and can discuss aspects of their past lives until an understanding is reached about what is expected for the next life. Achieved with love, compassion and the participation of the soul, it leads to the next physical incarnation having a purpose.

So how reliable is this information? Interlife regression has been progressively developed over the last 20 years, but particularly so over the last decade. The history is reviewed in the Appendix. Some of the pioneers include; Joel Whitton, Helen Wambach, Dolores Cannon, Peter Ramsden and Michael Newton. Many of them stumbled upon the interlife by issuing imprecise commands to a client during a past life, and amazingly found them talking about soul memories between lives. Thousands of people have now had their own interlife experience guided by the pioneers or other interlife therapists trained by them. The interlife reports show a remarkable consistency but what is particularly important is that many of the people in these interlife regressions had no prior knowledge. They also had beliefs from atheism through all the world's major religions. This is an important point to note, that the client's previous belief seems to make no difference to the nature of their interlife experience.

An area that needs to be discussed concerns subjective leading by the pioneers or interlife therapists. The narrative in the transcripts that have been used throughout this book will show the open type of questions that are used. Under hypnosis clients respond to questions extremely literally, much like a computer program. In other words, the client will only answer the question given. Deliberate falsification of information is virtually impossible, unless the client is not really in trance and a skilled therapist can tell when that is the case. A person in deep trance cannot just be directed to experience something unless they have the information to respond with. Most importantly much of the information is entirely new to the client yet relevant to their present life context.

Interlife testimony is consistent from what now amount to thousands of clients. The strength lies in that it comes from countless ordinary men and women. Many people think that this is the most profound source of spiritual wisdom that has ever been available to humanity.

The Mechanics of Interlife Regression
The techniques used in interlife regression are detailed in my book *Healing the Eternal Soul*. Let me take a moment to summarize how the process works. Hypnosis has traditionally been the approach to regress into past lives. Only a light level of trance is needed and this can be achieved with a short hypnosis induction, meditation or similar techniques. For an interlife regression clients need to be in a deeper level of trance, often the theta state that is experienced just before entering sleep. At this level the client's conscious mind is inactive and

their intuition link opens fully to the interlife memories. So the normal way of entering the interlife is from a past life while in deep hypnosis.

Of course the therapist needs to be able to assess the depth of trance and although this is not an exact science there are physical pointers. As a client goes deeper into trance their blood circulation slows and breathing becomes shallower. When talking there is a delay in answering questions and a literal response given. However, when a client starts to talk some trance depth is lost. Although it is possible to deepen the trance during the interlife, once the intuitive link has been established it tends to remain in place even for lighter levels of trance. The important thing for the therapist is to spot if a client has lost the intuitive link and drifted to a conscious level. This is achieved by checking for literal responses and assessing the quality of the voice. In some cases a client will even interrupt the session themselves to say that their conscious mind has become active.

The most common problem that can block an interlife regression is when a client does not achieve deep trance. Some 15 percent of the population can experience this difficulty. However, repeated exposure to hypnosis does deepen the experience and some clients benefit from using a self-hypnosis CD. Occasionally personal emotional issues arise and of course these need to be cleared before an interlife regression can take place. At a spiritual level a block can come from the client's spirit guide. Some or all of the interlife may be stopped because the clients conscious mind it not yet ready to receive the 'secrets of the soul'. To give too much information away would detract from their ability to use their free will in current life situations and learn from it. This tends to happen more for younger clients or those that are in the middle of a difficult life situation. Provided trance depth has previously been created and the intuitive link has been established, most sessions exploring the interlife can continue in excess of two hours without problems.

Progressing Interlife Research

I have now taken more than 160 people mainly from the UK, Germany, Holland and Scandinavia through interlife regressions. Twenty of these have experienced the interlife more than once, so that at the time of writing this book I have guided more than 180 sessions.

One consideration in picking the subjects for this type of research is to avoid criticism that the subject's previous knowledge had influenced the content of their interlife regression. This is particularly the case with Newton's interlife books that have sold in the hundreds of thousands and are widely available. So for this reason some of the subjects for the research were deliberately picked because they had not read any interlife or similar type of book. This was done through a questionnaire about their prior knowledge. Other considerations were to have written consent from each client to use their transcript, and the interlife content needed to be broadly representative of all the others.

Based on this information a final selection of 15 interlife cases were ranked into different categories. Five came from each of the following categories:

High: They had previously read about the interlife in some detail, and had retained a significant amount of that information.

Medium: They had previously read about the interlife some years ago and had forgotten the details.

Low: They had not previously heard or read about the interlife, or had very limited prior exposure.

We will see from the case study narratives in the book that the subjects with a high or medium level of prior knowledge sometimes came up with new information. This suggests their sessions could not have been totally influenced by their prior knowledge. Far more important, those who had no prior knowledge still described the same underlying elements of the experience. In fact some of the most interesting and detailed accounts came from these subjects.

The research approach that is used is different from other interlife pioneers. First, the subjects have come mainly from Europe rather than North America. Second, and more important each subject has been given a pseudonym and their narrative follows them through all the stages of the interlife experience. This allows for comparisons to be made between the different interlives to give a broader and more interesting presentation of the experience. The Appendix has a tabular summary that shows all the subject's personal details, the major elements of their interlife, and the order of these events. This approach also allows the subjects to give their feedback of the experience and its effect on them, which is shown in chapter 9. So using multiple subject narratives allows for a more in-depth presentation of this type of experience.

In order to enter their last interlife a client is normally regressed into their most recent past life. This enables them to benefit from the knowledge about planning for their current life and its purpose. If a client wants to experience more about this interlife on another occasion they can be guided to pick up the experience and further explore it. Of course if a different past life is used, the following interlife will then be different to the first interlife. To demonstrate this one of the subjects was given two interlife sessions from different past lives and the contrasting aspects examined. This provided a useful insight that has not been addressed before.

Sometimes when a client is regressed into a past life it may not be their most recent one. This sometimes happens when the client's higher self deems it appropriate. The past life that comes to the surface always seems to contain information more relevant to the client's current life. When this happens with a client I normally switch timeframes from the middle of one interlife with an instruction to move to the planning process in the most recent interlife. Then the client can benefit from finding out about the life planning for their current life. However for a few of the subjects in the book I deliberately left them in the original interlife to provide a research contrast. Again this is an advantage of using a narrative approach and has opened up new areas to investigate.

Hopefully these new approaches covering the experience itself, the presentation and the analysis, will build on the work of Newton and the other pioneers. It will also help to progress our collective understanding of what is in most cases a profound and moving experience.

The Presentation of Transcripts

Not all parts of the case studies have been presented because some parts were less detailed or revealing than others. Those that have been quoted make for the most interesting reading. Often my questions and the answers are shown in full, but where my questions are less important only the subject's answers are used. Any omissions are marked by dots. A difficulty with the subjects in trance is that they sometimes repeat themselves, and their grammar can be poor particularly for those who did not have English as their first language. So some minor adjustments have been made to improve the readability. For clarification I have occasionally added some of my own comments in square brackets. The overriding intent has been to present transcripts that are readable yet as accurate as possible to the original content.

1

TOWARDS THE LIGHT

Death is a favor to us
but our scales have lost their balance.
We are just a midair flight of golden wine.
Muhammad Hafiz, Persia, 14th Century.

What happens after death? Until recently humanity has relied on the various religious and esoteric traditions to provide the answers. The original purpose of these was to help the spiritual development of different cultures at different periods of humanity's history. At a deeper level they all have an important spiritual message that is very similar, often referred to as the 'Ancient Wisdom'. However, when it comes to providing information about what happens after death these traditions have unfortunately provided all sorts of contradictions and confusion. There are descriptions of heavens, hells, bardos, gods, angels, demons and the trials and tribulations to be overcome. The problem with many of these traditional views of death is that they contain widespread distortions however pure and wise their original sources might have been. Given these contradictions no particular tradition will be used for a comparison with the interlife experience.

However, it is useful to briefly mention near death reports. These often happen following a heart attack and last until the person is resuscitated. Considerable evidence has been accumulated from these experiences. A remarkable example is the research of cardiologist Dr Pim van Lommel and his colleagues from the Rijnstate Hospital in Arnham, Holland. They investigated the experiences of 344 heart patients resuscitated following a cardiac arrest over a 13-year period. All had been clinically dead at some point during treatment. Sixty-two of them reported a near-death experience, with 41 describing an experience which included traveling in a tunnel, reaching a light and meeting relatives. During their near death experience many patients had no electrical activity of the brain. This meant that their memory recall of near death experience could not be explained by traditional scientific explanations. Further investigation concluded that medical factors could not account for these experiences. Given the importance of this modern evidence a comparison between near death and interlife experiences will be included in this chapter.

The Three Realms

In the absence of consistency from the spiritual traditions a basic model has been developed to assist in understanding what happens after death. This can be thought of as containing three realms. It is perhaps useful to use the analogy of the different states of water when describing these realms, and their different energy levels. The densest level is the solid state of ice. When the vibrations of its energy increase the ice becomes water and eventually vapor. So relating this to the spiritual model, the densest spiritual energy is the physical realm in which we are all currently incarnated. The next higher level of vibration is the astral realm containing the spiritual energy that leaves the body after death. It's in this realm that trapped or earth-bound spiritual energy reside. The highest level of vibrational energy is what can be referred to as the light realm. This is what interlife regression or near-death subjects often refer to as 'the light' or 'home'. It is also here that the subjects describe meeting spirit guides, soul groups and elders.

It is not appropriate to think of the astral or light realms as having any location such as 'up there' and so on. Instead these realms can be thought of as occupying a different dimension of 'universal space' that is simply experienced. An analogy is a dream that cannot be said to exist in any one place but can be thought of as a dimension that we can never the less still experience. Another aspect of these two realms is the nature of time. No interlife subject reports on how much time passes for the simple reason that without a physical body subject to decay and death, time loses all meaning. So the actual interlife experiences may take seconds or years. All that is fixed in time is the point of leaving the physical body at death and the point of entering the baby for the next reincarnation.

To return to the question of what happens after death the following transcripts in this chapter and all the modern evidence point towards reincarnating human souls having only two main options after death. The first is that if they are severely confused or disoriented and retain a strong identification with people or places in the physical realm they may refuse to go to the light. Sometimes it may be because of unfinished business such as strong unresolved emotions of hate, love, fear, jealousy and revenge. If they have been unexpectedly killed such as in an accident or war they may not even realize that they are dead. Although they have obviously shed their physical body the spiritual body may exist in the astral realm for a varying length of time before realizing the predicament. Sometimes with the help of mediums or a spirit guide reaching out to them they return to the light realm.

The second option is that they enter the light realm shortly after death. Interlife evidence seems to suggest that the vast majority of souls do this. The only exception to this reincarnation cycle is when a soul has evolved sufficiently in karmic experience on the physical realm and has nothing to gain by returning to it. At this point there is still a variety of options for further spiritual development in the light realm.

So we have the physical realm that is the home of the physical body, the astral realm being a transitory state, and the light realm being the true home of all soul energies. Having established the context for interlife experiences, let us now turn our attention to the various elements.

Leaving the Body

All of the interlife pioneers report that the experience begins with the subject moving or floating out of their physical body after the point of death in a past life. They usually express a sudden sense of lightness and freedom, and sometimes the death scene is observed for a while with an air of detachment. Some even attempt with limited success to contact grieving friends and relatives, to give them comfort before they move on into the light.

Generally the subjects confirm these descriptions. Nicola Barnard, who had minimal prior knowledge of the interlife before her session, provides one of the most lucid accounts of departure. She has initially regressed to a scene in a past life in which she is a seated figure in a marble temple, when an earthquake suddenly brings it crashing down around her:

Go to the point where your heart stops beating and then tell me what happens?
There's a sense that it's me that's on the floor, and then there's me that's not on the floor anymore.
Have you left the body or are you still in the body?
I can see my body. I'm face down, but I'm dead. I can see my blood.
Are you able to describe the scene below you?
It's chaos, but the strange thing is it's not moving anymore. Everything's stopped. There's no more screaming or running around. So my body's lying face down on the stone floor, and rocks have hit me in the head. I feel very unconcerned. I'm not feeling distressed at all.
What happens to you next?

People have come to my body. They're very concerned and crying. They're very upset and frightened but I'm not there in it. I'm somewhere above it. I know these people, they're my friends. Somehow in all of this craziness, there's a kind of stretcher or something, and they're putting the body on it.

Ok, go to the point where you're ready to leave.

I'm not in the building anymore. There are big white clouds, and blue skies. It's by the sea.

Are you looking in the direction you're going, or are you looking back?

I'm high up, but I'm still looking down, and I can see the sea.

Do you feel any sort of pull or do you just know the direction to go in?

I'm aware that there are people who were my friends who are still on the earth. I'm just aware of them, it's not necessary to get closer.

Do you feel drawn to stay behind and see what happens to them, or can you move on?

I think I can go.

Ok, just describe your experience as you go.

It's a bit like a tunnel on the way in, although it feels very white to me. Almost like a tunnel that isn't dark at all, almost like it's made out of mists and things. It's funny because I'm walking, but I'm in the sky. There's no sense of physical support, but I'm walking rather than floating. I look the same. My hair is straight and I'm wearing the white gown and the sandals. I have some sense of these people living in little houses by the sea, and I feel very loving towards them. It's time to go and I get a sense that maybe I'm being drawn. It's almost as if I'm being called, but I can't hear anything. So it's more like a drawing, like a sort of pull. I'm sad, some part of me is sad to go. I'm still kind of lingering if you know what I mean. I love the sea. I really love the sea.

Nicola's slight reluctance to leave was presumably caused by the sudden and unexpected nature of her death. We will shortly find that this did not prevent her from moving into the light realms. Meanwhile another subject, Lene Haugland, adds an intriguing new dimension. She is describing how after a life as a Native American Indian woman who dies at the age of 72, she 'splits into millions of fragments' to ease the exit from the body:

I know what to do.
What is it you know what to do?
I have to go into small fragments, millions of small fragments.
Have you completely left the physical body?
Yes, and all these fragments have some sort of magnetic energies so they come together for a little while.
What starts to happen next?
It's like this pool of fragments goes into a stream of light, and it's kind of like a magnetic feeling, like I'm sucked into something.
What was the reason for being in millions of fragments?
That was my way to go out of my body. It's much simpler that way.
Are there other ways that you've come out of your body before?
Oh, I can go out in many different ways. One way is to take it out complete, but it's so heavy to do it that way. That is why I break up in all these fragments because it's not so heavy.
How do you make yourself go into all these tiny fragments?
I don't know, it just happens.

This description appears to be quite unique. However it does introduce an important concept that soul energy if split retains a link with each piece of itself and eventually reunites. This will be developed later in the book. Exiting the body is often far easier as illustrated by the report from Veronica Perry. She is an interesting subject because of the detail of her experiences despite her minimal prior knowledge. This is the second and shorter of her two interlife experiences from different past lives. She dies peacefully after a simple life and is surrounded by her sisters:

Go to the point that you take your last breath.
[Deep sigh].
And then tell me what happens.
[Sighs] I feel very light. I'm looking down at my body. My sister's sitting next to it. They'd prepared so well for my passing and everything's in place. It's like they're holding a space in the energy so that I can move on easily.
How are they doing that?
By focusing on love and peace, by joyously accepting the process. We don't mourn. We see it as a new beginning, not an end.
Is this helping you in any way?
I feel it's so easy to move on. I look and I can see so many souls trying to move on and they're being held back. Their loved ones want them to stay so much and they can't move on peacefully. I feel so honored that I'm allowed to move on so easily.
What do you experience next?
I just feel myself moving further and further away. I can see the bedroom and my sisters. Then as I move further away I can see so much more. I can see all over the land. I feel I'm being drawn away.

Here Veronica raises an important point. A soul's attempt to make the transition into the light after death can be hampered by the excessive grief of loved ones who do not want to lose them. This is often worse if they have no concept that the departing soul survives death and they will meet up again in the light realms. In most cases the grief will not actually prevent the soul from departing for the light unless it too cannot accept what has happened. In this wonderfully instructive case,

Veronica and her loved ones are fully prepared for her death. They even regard it as a celebration of her return to her true home, making her task that much easier.

Welcoming Parties

Other interlife research suggests that although more experienced souls may be perfectly happy to make the transition into the light alone, other souls are aided. This can be by a spirit guide or by already deceased friends or relatives from that life. Some of these may be members of their soul group with whom they will have shared many incarnations.

The subjects again corroborate this view. Liz Kendry describes being met by deceased family members after her death as a woman in her eighties as follows:

Just describe the scene below you.
I'm sitting in a wing chair with my head resting and it looks like I'm sleeping. The fire's still going.
Do you feel a need to stay with the body?
I'm going to go along with a tug. I turn away from the earth and look forward.
Tell me if you become aware of any lights in the distance.
Three. I'm moving towards them.
What do you start to notice?
I sense that one is my husband and the other two are my parents.
What happens as you make contact with your husband and parents again?
I'm not believing it. It's like a dream. Maybe I'm just dreaming.
Do they embrace you in any way?
Yeah.
Describe what it feels like when you're being embraced.
I feel surrounded by love. It's like they can wrap their whole

bodies around me.

This raises an interesting aspect of the initial transition that perhaps requires some clarification. The light realms can be perceived as 'a light' in near death experiences. In interlife experiences the light on closer examination always turns out to be one or more welcoming souls. Sometimes it may be whole clusters of souls. For Liz it is her husband and parents from that life who are her welcoming party. This is a fine example of the profound sense of love and comfort that characterize such reunions.

This is further demonstrated by Jack Hammond, who initially regressed to a relatively short life in which he was killed as a young soldier in WW2 while trying to save a friend. His spirit guide called Garth initially meets him, but then some of his soul mates decide to play a joke on him:

What does it feel like being in the presence of Garth?
Comfortable. Restful. Like you're supposed to be there. Like this is all supposed to be.
Ok, let's continue.
Um. I'm being left but I feel that I'm not alone. I'm with people.
Are these people in human form or energy form?
It's halfway, it's frustrating. If I were to put this in human terms, I'd say there's half a dozen people, shaded, with gossamer cloaks and hoods. Ah, no, they've taken them off now. They're laughing at me, smiling at me.
Was there any reason for them having these gossamer cloaks on?
[Laughs] They're playing a joke.
What's the joke?
How do I explain it? It's like they deliberately appeared in a way that I wouldn't expect. It's got something to do with my character- istics and my nature. Something like, 'you think you know it all,

but you don't, you see'. It's like I know them well. I couldn't say who they are in human terms, because they are dressed up.

What does it feel like being in their presence?

Ah, it's lovely. They're friends. We're embracing each other, smiling, laughing. They're thoroughly enjoying their joke.

Can they just change in whatever way they want?

Yes, I think that was the joke. They weren't in human form as such, they were in an energy form, which they'd made out to be these hooded mysterious-type people. That's obviously got some significance to me, like it's a joke on me. It's something to do with my ego, getting at my ego. They were sort of teaching me a lesson.

What sort of dialogue do you have with them after this initial introduction?

It's light hearted and not serious. It's not an in-depth discussion, it's almost like a welcoming committee, saying 'welcome back' and 'good to see you' and that sort of thing.

This case introduces another concept of the interlife. The perceived view of our spiritual bodies can change simply by the projection of thoughts into the energy. The normal soul body is of course just energy but it can be shown a human form for the benefit of the incoming soul. This will be explored in more detail later. In her first interlife session Veronica Perry regressed to the life of a woman who again led a simple life, and died in bed at the age of 86 surrounded by her family. On her departure from the body her spirit guide and a number of helpers meet her:

After you take your last breath what happens?

I can see seven beautiful lights coming towards me. [Sighs] They all come and envelope me. This beautiful warmth, it's like lying in the sunshine.

Do you know what's actually happening to you at the moment?

It's my spirit guides come to collect me.

Is this the presence that you can feel around you at the moment?

Yeah. It feels welcoming.

Is there any dialogue between you and your spirit guide?

He's just welcoming me back.

What are these other lights?

They are also guides and helpers.

What happens next?

They're moving me forwards and I'm leaving the room and leaving that body completely now. I take one last look back.

Tell me what you see.

It's like my friends and family are watching me go. They seem aware of my energy leaving and they're sad but they're happy too. I feel like I'm going with their love and their blessing and then I look forwards.

As you look forwards, what else are you aware of seeing?

My guides and helpers are all around. They smile at me.

Although the theme of loved ones not holding her back can be found in both of Veronica's sessions, it is clear that this is a substantially different transition. In this she meets guides and helpers at the time of the transition.

Returning to the narrative of Nicola Barnard, the victim of the earthquake. Eventually she leaves for the light realms despite her initial reluctance to leave her physical home by the sea. Her description highlights the important point of perceptions:

I can see flowers, and grass, and buildings maybe, but they are different from where I've just come from. They are simple and there's a different sort of quality about this place. It's lighter you know! It's as if everything is there and somehow not there. So even though they're buildings, they don't seem very dense... I think it's partly me creating them myself. It feels like when I focus on something, it's there.

All of the interlife pioneers report that in the light realms we can give our surroundings varying amounts of semi-physical form. This is achieved simply because energy follows thought. It often happens during the initial transition particularly for less experienced souls that need physical characteristics that will make them feel more comfortable and at home. It is why interlife sessions often contain various reports of huge crystalline castles, or green meadows and flowers. Sometimes the settings are described as classrooms and libraries, or perceived as temples with domes and columns. All these characteristics often contain elements of a favorite building or scene from the life on earth.

Welcoming souls project themselves in a form that will give comfort to those they meet, which is often as a family member or friend from the previous life. The more experienced souls are reasonably comfortable with meeting other souls and their surroundings in the natural energy form.

This is how Veronica Perry describes a spirit guide who meets her, just prior to receiving healing in her second interlife:

I feel he's actually a bit playful. I can see him in energy form, but I can also see the face of someone I would recognize in physical form. It's very, very bright, white light, and then as he shows me a more physical presence the colors that start off as very iridescent become deeper.

The Tunnel

Both Veronica Perry and Nicola Barnard previously referred to being 'drawn' towards the light, and most of the subjects talk in similar terms of being pulled by unseen forces towards it. This raises the question about the descriptions of traveling through a 'dark tunnel' and into the light that is so common with reports of near-death experiences. This rarely seems to happen in interlife regressions and most of the subjects did not mention the idea. Only Newton includes one published transcript that makes reference to a tunnel, but he also reports that most of his subjects merely see 'brilliant whiteness totally surrounding them at the moment of death'. Ramster explains his subjects occasionally experience, 'something resembling a tunnel or tube' and Fiore that, 'a few have experienced going through a tunnel with a light at the other end'.

Returning to the subjects. Liam Thompson found himself committing suicide as a young man in Ireland after his girlfriend had refused to run away with him because she had to tend to her sick mother. After his death he describes entering a 'black vortex, spinning away'. Wendy Simpson takes this description much further, and goes on to clarify the confusion about the tunnel experience. She initially regresses to the life of a poor man in the desert, who at the end is lying on a divan in a tent suffering from fever and tended by his wife and mother. After death the soul is unwilling to continue:

What happens as you take your last breath?
A sensation of looking down.
What can you see?
Just skin and bone.
Anything around the body?
Just the two ladies, and this feeling of attachment with the body.
What happens next?
It's like I'm suspended, I can't actually move.
Do you want to move on, or do you feel stuck?
I feel stuck for a while. It's like something letting go.
Do you know what is holding you?
It feels like a cord. I can still feel it quite deep inside.

What happens next?

It still feels a bit stuck.

Move on to the point where something else happens.

Now the suction is too strong, and the cord is getting thinner, and I'm being pulled up. It's like there is a tunnel of light.

Just describe this tunnel in a little bit more detail.

 I can see at the end there is bright light, and I'm moving through the dark part and coming out into the bright light. There is a sense of being met by beings. There is a sense of traveling.

At what point were you aware of the cord getting thinner?

Just before I went into the tunnel. It got thinner, and then I got sucked into the tunnel. Then I didn't feel the cord any more.

In near-death experiences and those who explore traveling 'out of the body' a cord that connects the soul energy to the physical body is often mentioned. This is however unusual in interlife experiences. Returning to the darkness of the tunnel under further questioning Wendy goes on to provide an answer about her experience:

It's because I was stuck. It was about not being able to let go, being trapped on the earth... The darkness of the tunnel represents the space between going and staying... It was fear that made me experience the darkness... To move on into the light I had to embrace the fear and accept it.

It appears that those who experience a certain degree of fear and confusion after death are more likely to sense darkness rather than light. This may well be true in near-death experiences, when people perceive that they are facing a sudden and unexpected death.

However is there more to the tunnel than this? One thing that should be remembered is that the experiences of near-death are different because the person is always turned back at the 'gateway' and forced to return. So perhaps their perception of a tunnel provides a guide that allows them not only to be drawn towards the light realms, but also to return from it.

This chapter has established that near death and interlife experiences do have similarities. They both describe leaving the body and being met by welcoming parties of departed friends, family, or by some a spirit guide figure. Although the black tunnel and cord are not often mentioned in interlife experiences, Wendy's case study provides a useful insight. Some people who experience a near-death may describe being met by an angel, or an identifiable prophet or god figure. Perhaps that person has a strong religious belief and these are energy projections from welcoming souls for the benefit of that person.

2

BECOMING WHOLE AGAIN

Those who don't feel this love
pulling them like a river.
Those who don't drink dawn
like a cup of spring water
or take in sunset like supper.
Those who do not want to change,
let them sleep.
Jelaluddin Rumi, Sufi mystic, 13th Century.

Healing

Some of the interlife pioneers describe an initial healing process for souls returning to the light realms. Ramster merely describes how souls seem to need an initial 'rest'. However, Newton reports more specifically that most clients receive a 'healing shower of energy'. The purpose is to remove the negative emotions and attitudes built up during the life just lived. Meanwhile, one of Cannon's clients describes a 'temple of healing' where 'waves of colored energies' pour over the soul.

Virtually all of the subjects confirm these standard ideas of energy healing in one way or another. The level of healing depends on the challenges of the life and the level of maturity of the soul. Usually they refer to the processes as washing away negative emotions and of expansion. An example of this is Laura Harper. Her healing follows a death as an old man looking after a young boy when ships invade their coastal town. She feels herself being 'wrapped' in a ball of 'swirling energy' with a 'pearl-like surface' that 'dissolves my unnecessary thoughts of sadness'. She has 'helpers who smooth or stroke the surface of my aura' so that 'all the parts of my body ripple like liquid'. Lene Haugland who was encountered previously splitting into millions of tiny fragments, also goes for healing. Still in a fragmented state she describes a 'stream of light' like a 'clean-up shower' that 'cleans out my feelings of sadness and loneliness'.

A particularly interesting case study is that of Nadine Castelle. After a life as a doctor in the US, she finds herself lying on her bed dying. Still in her fifties she is suffering an extreme fit of bronchial coughing. This can be clearly heard on the recording of the session, which shows just how real and immediate regression recall can sometimes be. She then proceeds with her transition, and for the first time a subject is presented discussing the idea that they can sometimes collect negative energies from others that need to be shed:

[coughing]

Go to the point of your last breath and tell what happens?

I've gone. I don't want to be in that body any more. I'm going up.

What's the next thing you experience?

One light is getting stronger and stronger coming towards me. It's enveloping me

What does it feel like?

I'm struggling to get rid of the heaviness of the body and shake it off. The light shining on me is a release. My energy is being restored, it's changing its configuration.

Have you changed configuration after other lives?

Sometimes.

In what way is this different?

I took on a lot of the energy and illness with me when I passed on, heavy matter. Now it needs to be shed because I don't want to take it with me. It's energetic particles from other people. I was suscep-tible to people's energy with my job. I'm in the light of healing and it's like resonating with the light.

Meanwhile, Liam Thompson who encountered entering a black vortex after his suicide, provides a vivid account of his healing as follows:

I'm going to be re-energized.

Well, just describe what happens.

It's like a shower with energy, pure energy. I can feel all the negative energy from my previous life going into a hole away from me. So it's a clearing out.

What does this hole look like?

It's more of a sensing.

Sensing that it's leaving you?

Yeah. It's going to be transmuted. There's no negative energy left. I've done this before, and I know what I'm doing.

Oh, have you done this after your previous lives?

Yeah. You normally do it after most lives. There's always some residue that needs to be taken care of. No one has a life with a clear straight road.

Just describe what you're experiencing and feeling.

Pure joy and love. It's like I'm an empty cup after the negative energy leaves and I'm being filled up with new energy. It's relaxing and everything's been washed away.

Magnus Bergen also provides an excellent healing account. He regresses to the life of an Italian man who repeatedly goes to prison for attempting to expose corruption in local government. During his first imprisonment his wife leaves him for another man, taking their son with her. By the time of his death of old age he is broken, lonely and depressed. He was not so much angry with his tormentors as frustrated by the dishonorable ways of the world. After his death he is not met by anyone, but soon finds himself in some sort of waiting room:

It's like I'm in a room with no walls.

What are you doing?

I'm passing through to go somewhere else. I still have the feeling of depression.

Go to the point where you leave this room, and describe what happens.

A door opens at the far end, into a hallway going upwards, it goes round and round. I'm not walking, I'm just following the shape.

Where are you now?

I'm in the right place. There are other energy forms trying to help me to make things better, to clear up and to work with my energies.

Tell me more about the experience?

It's gradually getting better and better. I have this feeling that these heavy energies are going. They are clearing up the depression and taking it away.

Are the vibrations of your energy changing?

Yes, definitely, it's becoming so much lighter. I feel like I'm becoming one of them because they are without any of these heavy energies.

Do you communicate with these others?

We don't really have anything to say to each other. It's not anything negative, it's just that being in their presence is enough.

The next three subjects all provide excellent, confirmatory accounts of the healing process, despite having minimal or no prior knowledge of the interlife. In her first session Veronica Perry's spirit guide and helpers lead her into a 'healing chamber' immediately after exiting the body:

Do you have any dialogue with your spirit guide?

He's asking about my energy, whether I still feel heavy or whether I'm starting to feel lighter now.

What makes you feel heavy?

Your energy has to be so heavy to be in physical form, to sustain that form, and until it's shed that heaviness there can still be a bit of confusion and disorientation.

So where do you go at this point?

Into the cleansing and healing chamber.

Just describe it.

So full of love and pure energies. It's like a bubble filled with love.

Do you always go here after other past lives?

There's always a need for some kind of healing, just to help the energy lift up. It's a big journey.

Are you by yourself?

I'm with my other guides and helpers. My spirit guide comes but he's not actively doing any healing.

Describe what it's like as that heaviness is taken away.

It's like being freed. I feel like I can shine now.

Was energy removed from you or added?

Some of the denseness that was left was removed, and that allowed my pure energy to grow. Although grow is not right, it's like it was restrained by the denser energy that had come with me, and now it's freed. It's like being able to stretch.

An interesting point here is that both Liam and Veronica suggest that all souls need some level of healing on entering the light realms. However, given the wide variety of lives and the maturity of souls there will always be exceptions. Later on in this session, Veronica also makes some insightful comments about the difference between the removal of excessive emotions and the retention of the associated memories:

The memories don't go with the cleansing, the cleansing just removes the heavier or more negative energies. Negative isn't the right word, but it's the only one I have. The more negative energies stop you being able to be in your soul form so they need to be lifted. The learning and the energy remain with you. They have to.

This is an important principal to remember that the memories of negative emotions carried from a life are retained in the light realms after the healing is complete. Even with the dense energy removed the issues from these unresolved memories will still need to be resolved by the soul in a future incarnation.

Delayering

The experience of healing is now taken further than the other interlife pioneers have explored. For the first time we encounter the idea of 'de-layer-ing'. Layers are removed in order to shed the heaviness of the earth realm. This account of healing is from a subject with minimal prior knowledge and comes from Nicola Barnard:

It seems to be clearing or cleaning me. It feels like there's some kind of healing property having this light shining on me... I like it. It's a nice feeling, it's shining all over my body... I'm becoming aware that I'm not so physical... There's a lot of love, I really feel a lot of love... It's like an electric blue light shining from the inside, it's amazing... I feel I have to let go of stuff... It's like letting go of an attachment to a physical body. It's funny because it's kind of going in layers almost. Now I feel more like a light, there's a gradual transition out of that sense of body. I can still sense myself as that person in the white robes with the hair and everything, but there's also a sense of this golden-pink light, and that is me too... There are different energies coming in, and it feels like all of these different colored lights are part of the healing process but they're beings, like me. I don't feel so upset any more. There's a sense that what I was doing in that life was quite difficult… Although I really got a strong sense of tranquility and balance from it, there's also some sense of remorse at not being able to save people from the suffering but it's lighter now, it's definitely lighter.

It's useful to remember that Nichola Bennet's healing followed dying in an earthquake buried under rubble. When she says 'there's a gradual transition out of that sense of body' it would appear that she is describing the delayering of the physical dense energy from that traumatic death.

Veronica Perry's second interlife session provides an excellent description of delayering. In contrast to Nicola Bennet's report she describes it as traveling through different layers. She also becomes aware of the presence of her spirit guides. The playful one reported on in the previous chapter, and another teacher:

I feel like I'm floating. Floating through all these different colors and layers of color.

Do you know what they are?

I feel that they're somehow preparing me, helping me to shed the different aspects of life that I can't take with me. I feel like they're preparing any residue of physicality that I bring with me, any links to my body. It's part of a healing process, but I seem to be just visiting each layer and moving on very quickly.

Are you doing this by yourself?

I feel I'm being guided.

Are you able to see who is guiding you?

I've got two energies, one to the left of me and one behind me. We're not speaking or communicating at all, but they're guiding me through.

What is being attended to in each of these layers?

I've moved through quite a few now, but I'm looking back at the first layer and it seems quite dense. Although when I went through it felt very free and light, it's a very physical layer.

Was something being added or taken away?

That was a cleansing away of any physical attachments, any remainders of physical energy, that needed to be shed.

Were any emotions removed from you at that point?

I feel that there wasn't very much removed. There was some sort of a connection with my sisters. Although they were easing my transition and my process, I also had to release my connection to them. They weren't holding onto me, but I was still holding onto them a little.

What happened in the second layer?

The second layer starts to work on the more energetic level. Not so much the physical attributes, but more the emotional and spiritual holdings-on to that life. I feel that I had such a deep love and connection to the earth and to nature, some of which is a part of my soul, but there are parts of that connection that needed to be shed because they were more linked with the physicality of that life. I feel that there was so much peace and understanding and accep-tance in that life that there doesn't seem to be any emotional baggage that needs to be shed. There weren't any real ailments, or illnesses, or pains, or physical problems that need to be shed. I feel that in going through these layers of healing and cleansing my soul energy is being tweaked back into balance. It's more the vibration of my energy that needs to be raised and just a few little bits cleansed here and there. It's a transition between the denseness of the energy that's needed in physical form and the lightness that is needed here.

What level are you at now?

I'm towards the end of this healing process and looking back on what's been done. I'm in a very, very light space. My guide's with me and I almost feel like I'm in a resting space.

Veronica then goes on to describe in some depth how her spirit guide and teacher assist in the whole process:

It's like I've got two very different characters with me. I've got the one who I feel I know very well, and who is a bit playful and there's an excitement to be with each other. The other is very much more quiet and guiding, like a silent guiding force.

What role does this other one play?

I feel she's quite important. For me, she's a teacher.

Was your teacher doing the healing in the different layers?

Sometimes being in the energy of that layer would be enough and when where things needed to be tweaked or released, she was coming forward to help. She would just pick things out, discard the things that weren't needed anymore. I could feel my energy becoming whole, and complete and purer. Where the little bits were being removed, the energy of the layer I was in swelled to fill that gap, and I just felt more and more whole. It's difficult to put into words, but it's like the more that was removed, the bigger I got.

She concludes by specifically confirming that the healing required and the particular souls who come forward to help in the process are dependent upon the life just lived:

There are different experiences at the end of every life, dependant upon what happened in that life…This one is easier because I've transitioned from one peaceful, loving, healing place to another. In lives where there's been trauma this transition is much more difficult because there's so much residue of energy coming through. I'd worked to shed a lot of that energy in that life, so there was less to bring through to be healed. In traumatic lives, this is the first place where that healing can start taking place, so it's much harder and the levels seem very different.

When you've had past lives with traumas, was it always the same teacher and spirit guide that helped with your healing?

I've had other spirits of light helping me with different things. There is a group that oversees your choices, and your lives, and your learning. Some are drawn to guide you in different experiences, or you're drawn to them.

The impression from this account is that the more experienced teachers normally associated with the life review and planning might also be involved in the initial healing process. Although this is unusual, it suggests that the distinction between spirit guides, teachers and perhaps elders may be rather more fluid and less well defined than the other interlife researchers have suggested. Given their widespread role to assist our development this should come as no surprise.

Equally revealing is the information provided by David Stephens, who regressed to the life of a young Arab man who is robbed by bandits and left to die. He is buried in the desert sand, the sun beating down and his lips cracking like sandpaper. He seems to have been able to make the transition entirely alone:

Go to the point your heart stops beating for the last time and tell me what happens.

I feel cool and look down. Sand is being blown across my half-buried body, and I stay a while until the sand covers it. Part of me still feels angry about what happened. I know I need to carry some of that anger with me when I go.

Are you leaving any of that anger behind?

Some of it stays, but some I need to take with me otherwise it will carry on to the next life. The body is buried now, and I'm ready to go. It's like the dawn. I move like a rocket.

Are you able to choose how much anger to leave behind?

Yes.

How much do you decide on?

About a quarter. Now I have the anger but it does not have me.

Do you know what will happen to the part left behind?

It will stay with the person who harmed me. We were robbed. There was a group of us, and they were bandits who left us to die.

What purpose will it serve?

I feel like saying revenge, but there is a deeper purpose than that. It's a reminder to him, an opportunity for him to learn and grow, to realize the consequences of his actions.

Is this a decision you make alone?

We decided on this before. He is a younger soul and not aware of the consequences. He will have a hard life now, it will not be easy. Every time he hurts someone, this will remind him.

This is a fascinating insight, that what appears to be a relatively experienced soul can make a deliberate decision about the element of emotion to leave in the physical realm and the amount to take into the light realms. It is certainly not something that has been previously published in interlife material. We will find that it forms something of a counterpart to the deliberate process of choosing what emotions to bring back into incarnation. It is also interesting that David reports that the whole process was preplanned.

His transition then continues, and again he finds himself traveling rapidly through layers to shed 'skins' and 'heaviness':

It's like being shot out of a cannon. As I fly up through the different layers it's like shedding skins. The heaviness starts to go. I'm holding the anger and pain like cradling an infant. Ah, I see now. I could easily have left all of it, but then it would have formed an attachment.

What difference is there between the part you left behind and an attachment?

The part I left is thoughtful, wise anger. The part I'm taking is the vengeful anger, the blind rage, the despair. The earth does not need any more of that, and I know where it needs to go. There is a pool that I can create.

Are you at this place?

Yes.

Please describe it.

I choose it to look like a pool in a jungle by a waterfall, with fishes in it.

Have you created these thought-forms yourself?

Yes.

What do you do in this place?

I swim to an island in the middle with this bundle of anger and start to work with it to release, to smooth and untangle. It's like grooming an animal that has dried mud on it, and its hair has got tangled.

Do you do this work yourself?

Yes. It's quite easy. It reminds me of who I truly am.

What is going to happen to the energy you are removing?

Once it's been cleansed and straightened I'll draw it back into myself again and use it to add perspective to memories from that life.

It will be fast becoming clear that at a soul level David is far more experienced than most interlife subjects in dealing with the healing process. This is something he is perfectly comfortable tackling on his own despite having had a traumatic death:

Is this something you have done previously after other lives?

Yes.

Is this something you have had special training in?

Yes. I've worked with others as well.

Can you tell me more about this work?

It's joyful. When the one who caused my death in that life finishes I'll help him. It's like, I'm finding the words hard, it's like a cleansing, nurturing, releasing. It's even more of a joy working with others than with my own energy.

How does this process of clearing energy work?

I can see the energies of the whole person, and just after they die it's like a tangled knot. It's just like a knotted ball of string inside them, and together we draw it out and I help them untangle it. There's something very intimate about it. It needs a lot of mutual trust and sensitivity. You cannot just grab hold of it and tug it, you have to understand what the strands are, each one is a feeling or thought. All the fears, anger and pain. That's why I left some with him, so I can work with it when his life ends.

Do you do this work with other souls?

It's not my job. It's not what I do all the time, but it's something I can do with those I work directly with.

Are there other souls who specialize in doing this work all the time?

Yes. Not all the time. They have other things too, but they work quite intensely with this. They work with lots and lots of other souls.

Is there a name for doing this work?

They are called healers.

So now we realize that David has trained as a healer. It is fascinating that he should have chosen to work with a less experienced soul who he had preplanned would murder him. Also he deliberately left certain emotional energies to assist their learning. Finally after the death of his murderer he came back to help with their healing.

A general observation from these various accounts of delayering and healing is the confirmation that souls personalize the energy of their surroundings that best suits them. Some describe healing showers of energy that may be in semi-physical places such as a temple or hospital. Others have quite unique and individual experiences. The descriptions and indeed the experiences themselves, vary according to the experience of the soul. Its also varies with their personal preferences, the extent of trauma in the last life, and the extent of assistance required from others.

Veronica Perry and Liam Thompson indicated in the previous extracts that all souls would go through the healing process to some extent. It is probably safe to assume that the same basic healing process is at work for all souls, but the description of delayering is a more complete description of the process. The first energies being unraveled are the heavier, physical energies that are discarded, followed by emotions and other energies so that the soul can operate effectively in its new lighter surroundings. Looked at in this way, it becomes clear that delayering is the essential process that brings about the profound change required to switch from the physical realm to soul consciousness in the light realm. A soul would simply not be able to resonate with the higher vibrations of the light realms without it.

Dealing with Trauma

Newton suggests that the healing process is far more intensive for souls who have had more traumatic lives. He describes what appears to be a sort of emergency treatment center for seriously traumatized souls. Here they are 'reshaped' or even 'remodeled' via transfusions of pure, new soul energy. He also suggests that in cases of milder trauma souls may still require considerable reorientation in the form of an initial past-life debriefing with their spirit guide, in addition to any energy healing they might receive. One of Cannon's subjects refers to a 'special place for damaged souls to go to rest and restore themselves'.

The subjects fully corroborate and add to this assessment. There is David Stephens' testimony from the last section concerning the 'energy unraveling' activities of specialist healers. Also Veronica Perry continues her second interlife account with an in-depth description of how she too helped in the emergency debriefing of a severely traumatized soul. Of significance is that her prior knowledge was only a very different first interlife session. It is so revealing that the narrative is offered in full:

I'm seeing a soul who has just passed, and I go to help him. He has just left his body and he's still very attached to the physical. I go to help guide him to the light, because he's finding it hard to find it. He's actually very, very angry because he didn't want to leave. So I go and I take his hand and I try to give him all the love that I can, but in doing that I also need to be very harsh and firm with him. I tell him that he has passed, and that he needs to come to the light, where he will find everything he needs. I have to be very stern with him, and he eventually lets go and comes to the light. The first level of healing for him is very, very hard. Almost traumatic to watch.

How is it actually done?

There is a group of us, seven. This soul needs a lot of healing. We almost treat him as though he's in physical form, because he still sees himself in physical form and still feels very physical. He's brought so much with him that his energy is still very solid. So we have a table, and instead of him feeling that he's passing through different levels of energy, for him this level is a room with a table.

Are the room and table created for him, or does he do this himself?

It's something that we create together with him. It seems that both he, and we as his helpers and guides just know what is needed. We don't even need to think about it.

Then what happens?

We're all standing round him and we're giving him healing. Before we can help him to release any residual energies and negativity, we need to raise his energies up a little. When you're in physical form you have an aura, and his aura, his energetic body, is tightly packed and condensed. It's so tiny that even though he is in energetic form now he's still almost solid. That has made it hard for him to release anything. So we have to try and raise and soften his energies so we can start getting in there. It's like the difference between trying to cut a piece of steel and trying to cut a piece of cheese. It's hard to get in there without it being softer so we give him energy. We channel energy for him so that he can start to relax a little and this process can start to take place. He's had a very difficult life.

What sort of trauma did he have?

He was abused as a young child very violently by an uncle and he became vengeful, aggressive and violent as a result. He not only needs to deal with the abuse that he suffered himself, but also the abuse he then inflicted on others - his own aggression and violence. It's very traumatic for him.

What do you do?

We've managed to get his energies to relax a little. He needs a lot of love, which I feel is one of the reasons that I'm here. I feel that I need to channel a lot of love to him so I do. That's to help him get to a space where he can start to look at some of the things that happened in that life, and start to deal with some of the issues.

Does he have to re-experience some of those aspects of that life as part of the healing?

Yes, he does.

How does it happen?

Through experiencing some of the events that took place again. In this place of deeper understanding he is able to start to let go of some of the things that his energies have been holding onto so strongly.

Does he get more insight here than when he was on the earth realm?

Yes. He's able to see more of the bigger picture of what's happening and to look at things not only from his own perspective, but also from the perspective of others that were with him in that life. He gains a level of understanding of what took place.

When people on the earth realm re-experience events it can be extremely emotionally intense. Is it the same in the spirit realms?

It's very different. It would be wrong to say that there's no emotional release. There has to be and that's one of the things we're looking to achieve in this process. He needs to release the emotions, the anger and the fear, because they are all dense emotions that are not needed and will only serve to hinder his soul energy. Although there is the intensity of release it's not felt in quite the same way. In human form the emotions are everything as you're releasing them, they're in every part of you. In soul form, what he's feeling is a precious freedom as he lets go of those intense, dense emotions. It's like me telling you about the little bits of energy that were being released from me as I was moving through the levels, and the intensity of the feeling was my energy being able to expand into its proper form. For him, it's the same thing as those emotions, those intense feelings, are released. The intensity that he is feeling is his soul energy expanding, and being able to expand.

What happens to him next?

After each layer of release he has a lot of healing.

Just go through those layers for me.

The second layer is more of a peaceful cleansing.

How you do that?

Again, there are still seven of us with him, but we no longer need the room and the table. Here he needs to rest in the cleansing energies that are around him, helping him to finish with the trauma he went through in the first layer.

Does he move onto other layers?

Yes. Although he has released and cleansed the emotional attachments of the traumatic events, his energies need to be fine-tuned. He was holding onto so much.

Are you involved in this fine-tuning?

No. I know I have been at other times, but not on this occasion.

When you have been involved, what do you do?

I see lots of symbols, and different colors of healing light. I can see somebody standing underneath these healing light energies and they are washing over them. At the same time where there are gaps and spaces, it's helping the soul to fill them.

Are these energies of different vibrations in the other levels?

Yes. Very, very high vibrational energies. You stand away from them if you don't need them.

Is moving through these different layers like moving from one place to another in the spirit realms?

Yes. It's like moving from the entrance of the spirit realm through to the spirit realm itself, but it's only the start.

This is clearly a hugely important account, for a number of reasons. It specifically supports the suggestion that delayering is the fundamental process involved in all transitions. It confirms that there is interplay between spirit guides and the newly arrived souls in creating an appropriate perception of their environment. In this example the room and table were created as the perception of the first level of healing by all those involved automatically and without thought or effort. Lastly it supports the idea that healing can involve an element of past-life review, especially with more traumatized souls.

Special Rest

Although there is clearly a general similarity and overlap between the ideas of resting and healing, it seems that more traumatized souls may also need an extra period of rest and recuperation. The main example of this is Liam Thompson, and although we have seen that his initial healing seems to be relatively straightforward, his soul was clearly traumatized by his recent suicide. As a result he reports that he takes some time out for special rest, although in fact he delays it until various other transitional processes have been attended to:

What do you do next?
Rest.
Where do you go to do this?
A place where energy encompasses you, like a warm blanket.
What's the purpose of this rest?
To completely rejuvenate. Sometimes people stay here for long periods of time, depending on how severe their life was before.
Is this resting associated with the severity of your last life?
Yes. The re-energizing normally does most of it when you first come back.

Reintegrating Soul Energy

Deliberate decisions are made about how much soul energy is brought into incarnation when returning to the physical realm. This enables some energy to merge with the physical body and the remaining soul energy to continue to operate in the spirit realms. So when re-entering the light there is need to reunite with the soul energy left behind. This aspect is really only explored in detail by Newton. He emphasizes that souls can choose the timing of the process for themselves. Sometimes they undertake it during the initial healing and reorientation phase, but more often on their return to their soul group.

Again the subjects confirm this. Katja Eisler regressed to a past life of a Mexican peasant with more regard for his donkey than people. After being struck by lightning, she has various past-life reviews and meets up with her soul group before receiving healing, helped by her spirit guide Merlo:

What does Merlo say?
He asks me if I want to go to a kind of restoration room.
Describe what happens when you get there.
It's a small wooden building and it's glowing. I'm going inside and there's a shower in there. It's made of energy but I can see the form, it looks like I could touch it but it's glowing.
What happens next?
I take a kind of a shower under this fluid energy. I am getting a bit lighter and there's a tingling in my hands, but there's still pain in my arms. I can see the glowing drops of energy. They are washing away all the old debris.
How do you feel?
Everything is moving faster now, I feel stronger and more as one than before.
Have you connected with your soul energy yet?
No. We're flying outside. I see part of my energy, it's like a flame and it feels good to see it.
Is this the energy you left behind?
Yes. I certainly know it's mine.
How do you know it's yours?
Because I can feel the connection, an invisible connection and it's like a rope.
How do you reconnect with this energy?
We are merging. I feel stronger, much stronger and more confident.

Liam Thompson, following his past life suicide, only reintegrates after healing and at the end of his long rest period:

Have you joined with the rest of your soul energy yet, or is this still to come?

It's coming now.

Just describe how it happens.

My guide, it's like he's holding a jar, but it's not a jar. Inside it's like a light and that's my energy. I feel my energy is pulsating. He knows where it needs to go. It's like a magnet. He releases the lid and that's it. Joined.

And what does it feel like?

Empowering. Very empowering. I didn't take enough energy when I went to earth. Hmm.

Although she has some initial healing as described previously, Lene Haugland too goes off to visit various libraries before deciding to reintegrate describing it as like being inside 'a spinning ball of intense energy with small fragments of light going through me'. She also explicitly confirms that it was her choice to leave reintegration this late and not do it before visiting the library. Meanwhile in her first session Veronica Perry confirms the extent of choice in the timing:

Have you merged with the other part of your soul energy yet?

Yes, I've merged with it as part of the healing and cleansing, but in previous times I've done it at different stages.

What has happened on these previous occasions?

At these previous times I've had to be cleansed, and then healed, and then merged. This was quite a pure life so it could be done in one go. The energies that I've bought back with me weren't too heavy or too interfering.

What does it feel like to be cleansed and merged with your soul energy?

I feel very light, and whole. It's good to be back.

Despite these apparent reports of variable timing, it is quite clear that soul reintegration is a further extension of the whole healing, lightening and delayering process. The reason for the occasional delay in merging with the core soul energy is offered by one of Newton's subjects. He reports that they sometimes prefer to focus on the life just lived for a while especially during any reviews, before allowing their full soul perspective to come into play.

3

REVIEWING PAST LIVES

If you look for truth outside yourself
it gets farther and farther away.
Today, walking alone,
I met him everywhere I step.
Only when you understand it this way
will you merge with the way things are.
Tung-Shan, Chinese Zen Master, 9th Century.

Nearly all the traditional religious approaches contain some idea of the departed soul being judged after death. The ancient Egyptians were obsessed with ensuring that they would gain a favorable ruling when they came to the 'Judgment Hall of Osiris' and their heart was 'weighed in the balance'. This would ensure their soul's immortality because an adverse ruling would necessitate its destruction. Indeed the elite of their society spent considerable sums having inscriptions on the walls of their tombs and their sarcophagi that contained all the spells they would need to pass the ultimate test.

At least in Ancient Egypt they had a sense of how to draw things to a conclusion, with unworthy souls destroyed. By contrast, their Mesopotamian counterparts believed that those who obtained an adverse judgment from the gods who 'decreed their fate' were destined to live on in the 'netherworld', in a kind of gray limbo state. Even worse, by the time their influence had filtered down through Judaism and into the Christian Church, we find that unworthy souls are condemned to everlasting torment. It seems that the primary motivation for this development was not new spiritual insight, but instead the desire to keep the uneducated masses under control. After all, what could be more successful than to threaten them with eternal damnation and torment if they stepped out of line?

So what is the reality of the situation as suggested by interlife evidence? The answer from all the pioneers and from the subjects in this book is that we are not judged. The past life is reviewed, often with the help of other souls to assist. They merely provide comfort, perspective and clarification.

Soul Perspective

The previous chapter highlighted how the whole of the transition and healing process is intimately connected with the life just lived and the emotions it generated. Some souls may need emergency debriefing that involves an element of past-life review. So Veronica Perry's traumatized charge needed 'help to get him to a space where he could start to look at some of the things that happened in that life, and start to deal with some of the issues'. Connected to this was the idea that his soul was suddenly able to experience his actions from a far broader perspective: 'He's able to look at things not only from his own perspective, but also from the perspective of others that were with him in that life.'

Whitton reports that 'any emotional suffering that was inflicted on others is felt as keenly as if it were inflicted on oneself'. Newton provides the case of Unthur who in his review is 'mentally placed back into the body of a smaller child he bullied in a school yard in his past life, and allowed to feel the same pain he caused'.

The concept of quite literally experiencing it from the other person's perspective is corroborated in some reports of near-death that can contain elements of life review. So the soul perspective that this chapter covers is the past life review of how our actions and thoughts effect not only ourselves but others too. This is a depth of review that has more insight than anything we might normally achieve consciously while alive.

Solitary Reflections

Some souls seem to understand the true nature of their mistakes after death. Although this can introduce new tensions, in most cases these seem to be relatively short-lived because spirit guides are soon on hand to help put everything into proper perspective.

David Stephens seems to have been sufficiently experienced to do it himself. He also sorts out the emotional issues from his life as the Arab man left to die in the desert in the initial healing process that he conducted himself. The same appears to be true of Lene Haugland after her life as a Native American Indian woman dying of old age. Nicola Barnard who is killed violently in an earthquake reports feeling quite serene about her death after her healing. So it appears that the healing process may be enough for some souls without the need to engage in a detailed life review at this point.

The suggestion that we are our own harshest critics comes from the experience of Lisbet Halvorsen. She regresses to a life as a ship-owning slave trader operating in the central Mediterranean, who dies aged 60 in his cabin from a smoking-related lung problem. She experiences immediate and profound regret about a life of such emptiness and materialism:

I immediately regret this pathetic life… I want to get away quickly… I feel so ashamed… That was a terrible life… I'm alone now, just feeling the shock of how easy it was to lead an empty life. How easy it was just to go with my instincts and be completely cut off. How easy it was to be self-satisfied. I felt I did nothing wrong at the time, and now there's this light ahead of me and I'm thinking 'how was it possible to be so cut off from love, and not be critical of myself at all?' I think quite a few people that I know in this life were with me, and I was the leader, leading them all to be so stupid. I was manipulative with my words, and we all believed we just did what we had to do.

In an unusual turn of events, she then thinks she is having a life review with her spirit guide but he turns out to be a soul mate. We also find that her regret turns to irritation when she remembers that she previously agreed to take on that life as part of some kind of experiment:

My life review goes quite quickly... I'm talking to my teacher now, this older person, someone I trust and who understands me. He's saying 'so how did you think that was?' I say 'I didn't think it was possible to go down and have a life not remembering the important things', and he is saying 'see, it's that easy to forget'... Actually I'm a bit angry because I feel that I was tricked. It's like there was a bet and I was feeling so wise. Actually he's not my teacher, he's just a friend. He was saying 'you think you're so wise, if the conditions are like this and that, then it is possible to lead such an empty life'. I took on the challenge and I proved it, and now I'm angry... I was not centered, not in connection with my feelings. I just went with my intellect... It was so empty and I'm annoyed that I had that life. He's laughing at me, not being mean, he's just saying 'you see?'

Lisbet's experience provides us with an important reminder of just how easy it is for us to ignore our intuitive, spiritual side, when we are immersed in the daily life of the physical realm. However the one saving grace for her is that her former personality intuitively recognizes a slave who he saved and took as his wife. It appears that this main positive element of that life was planned in advance:

The only time I connected was when I saved that woman. That was the one thing I was supposed to do, and I did it.

We might recall Magnus Bergen's life in Italy, who is jailed unfairly for the things he says. He conducts his life review entirely alone, although unlike Lisbet it occurs only after he has been healed and reunited with his soul group. He offers an inspirational insight that he retains no anger towards his persecutors. This is despite paying a huge and tragic price for remaining a man of principle and experiencing extreme sadness and depression on his deathbed. It also seems that the frustration he had with the human world at his death has now been translated into a soul perspective that he refers to with even more detachment:

> I'm glad that it's done. I see how much sadness there was in that life... The best thing was that I followed what I believed to be right, and kept faith in working for a good cause. I see that I was strong in not giving up or being intimidated... But the downside was simply how it was to be a human being in that place. How it was to experience all those hard feelings of separation from my son and wife. Of being locked up in jail, and all the sadness in my last years after there was nothing left to live for and my work was done.

Spirit Guide Reviews

Solitary reflections of the type just discussed seem to be relatively rare. The majority of the subjects found themselves reviewing the past life with their spirit guide. These are evolved souls that will have been involved in the subject's life plan and overseeing it from the light realms.

Sometimes these reviews occurred after healing and sometimes after they had been reunited with their soul group. As we will start to discover with the rest of the interlife experiences there is fluidity in the order of events rather than them always occurring in a specific sequence.

Veronica Perry who has minimum prior knowledge provides an excellent description of her review with her guide, Hathwar. It is not a lengthy or complex process because she has just left a simple life with few complications. However she does provide excellent descriptions of the different review methods available. She perceives her environment as a 'big dome full of sparkling crystals':

We're going on to talk about that life.

Does this review start at the beginning of the life or the end?

We're sort of watching it from the beginning.

How are you watching it?

We've chosen to watch it on a big screen.

What other choices could you have had?

I could've chosen to view it telepathically, and we could've chosen to relive it and stop at the pertinent times.

What made you decide to watch it on a screen?

I find it more relaxing.

Have you ever chosen to relive it?

Yes.

What was the reason for that?

On that occasion the physical and emotional aspects of the life I had just lived were very important for my soul growth. There were some very big lessons to be learnt from that life, and I needed to integrate them properly into my energy system.

Ok, just tell me what happens in your review of this life?

We're watching it on the screen. It goes very, very quickly. My spirit guide is asking if this was a good, restful life.

What do you say?

Yes. I'm really grateful to have had this life, it was almost like a holiday.

What was the purpose of this life?

It was about reconnecting with nature, and the peace and the love that it's possible to experience in physical form. It was also about being able to be a pure and aware channel for the higher vibration energies to come through.

Just summarize briefly what happened to you.

I was born into a good family. My mother was a Wiccan and she taught me 'the ways', and I passed them onto my daughter and son. My husband was a good man. I was surrounded by loving people, and enjoyed everyday life. I enjoyed my relationships and I enjoyed my family. It was simple and wasn't a wealthy life, or a life full of riches and glamour, but it was a life free of trauma and pain.

Is there any discussion with your spirit guide about the sadness of leaving people at the end of that life?

I don't feel that now. The sadness was just because I loved them so much. I liked watching them grow and their lives changing, and them blossoming into the people they were meant to be. I know that I can watch that from here.

This provides another important reminder to us all, that the simple things in life are far more fulfilling than material wealth and power. Veronica's own attitude towards the friends and family she has left behind is just as exemplary as their attitude to letting her go with their blessing on her death. Corroboration of Veronica's three methods of review; screen, telepathy with her guide, or re-experiencing the events, is provided by Nadine Castelle:

I'm supposed to go and review that life... My guide Anrian will come with me... It's a room with tables, lots of people sitting down and the tables are long... It's kind of a concave room with rings of light making an enclosure... You can see it as whatever you want to see it as. I see it as energy... There are other energy forms learning about their own past lives by review... I'm doing mine by myself... It's to see if I'm satisfied... I can see it in whatever form I want to take it in. I can either review what my life was, or feel what is was, or energetically connect with that life to see if it matched up with what my intentions were... My guide is with me to make sure I'm in the right space, and to help me if I need help. I know if there is something I should have done that didn't match my original intentions.

It is probably fair to assume that 'reviewing the life as it was' is the equivalent to Veronica's screen, 'feeling the life' is equivalent to a telepathic review, and 'energetically connecting with the life' is equivalent to a full re-experiencing of it. Nadine then continues by revealing how she did not completely fulfill her own plan in that life as a doctor:

I was able to fix the energetic configurations of people's bodies when they were ill... I wasn't allowed to say what I was doing. In that human form you don't really know, you just feel it. I was doing it but there was missing information and that was not according to my intentions... My intentions were to fully realize my abilities... Sometimes the negative energy from a wound got stuck on me and I didn't know how to clear it.

Here she is again referring to the energy attachments from her patients that she had to shed on transition. However it is not her inability to avoid these in that life that seems to concern her now. It is not having been able to fully utilize her soul's knowledge of how energetic healing really works. She concludes her review with some pointers for her future work in both the light and physical realms:

I need to continue to work with awareness of energy fields and how they affect physical matter in the future... There was no awareness then, and that's why I was confused.

The Library of Life Books

In the previous extract Nadine has already specifically confirmed that souls can choose to perceive their surroundings for the life review in whatever way suits them best. This equally applies to all events in the light realms. One setting favored by a number of the subjects is a library.

A good example of this comes from Marta Petersen, who regressed to a past life as a young Jewish girl in Warsaw during WW2. Her review with her guide Fallon commences with a description of a library setting:

I have to go to my study home to meet my guide.
Just describe what it's like.
It's very secluded, but I don't have to go very far if I need something. It looks like an old library from Greece with big pillars outside. It's white, and there's some big stairs leading up to the main entrance. It looks like it has a roof on it but when you're inside you can look straight up.
Describe the meeting with your guide.
He meets me just inside. He has a big white robe on, like he hides his energy. This is for me I know.
What is the name of your guide?
[Pause] Something with an 'm'. [Pause] It cannot be pronounced…
His nickname is Fallon.
Ok, well tell me what happens in this review.
We go down another hallway and we're going to sit in the garden, under the tree, because this is where I love to sit.

A regular feature of the description of library review settings is that they contain 'life books'. Marta now turns to hers, revealing that they can come alive similar to mini film screens:

> I go back into the study hall and there's a book waiting there for me. It has my name on it.
> *And what is it about?*
> It has my old lives in it.
> *And how do you go about reading this book?*
> My name is spelt backwards. I read it from right to left.
> *Why is that?*
> I'm not sure, this is just how we read it.
> *How does the book work?*
> When I open it it's like little movies, and I just have to concentrate on what I want to see and then it appears to me.

As she continues we find that her reason for consulting her life book is that she wants to examine certain threads that have connected many of her past lives, and also their implications for her next one:

> I'm concentrating on the fact that I have worked alone most of my lives.
> *Has this been a problem, or something you enjoy?*
> Usually I enjoy it, but it gets kind of lonely and I think it's time for me to work more closely with others, because we are more powerful when we work together.
> *Have you finished with the book now?*
> Yes.
> *Is there anything else that comes to mind?*
> The next life I'm going to have is going to be more demanding, and it's not going to be like the one I just had where I was there for another person.
> *And do you know about what areas you want to work on?*
> I want to do something creative where I can reach most people, so

I thought about painting but my experience with that is not as great as with music.

So you could reach lots of people with your music?

I tried this before. This is what I do best.

Liz Kendry provides a rather more depressing account of her review in the library with her guide, Inka. We now find that despite her longevity in her previous life, she gave up after the death of her beloved husband:

I'm in a huge library with lots and lots of books.

Who's in this place with you, is it just you and Inka?

There's other people milling around, but he takes me to a table and that's where we sit.

How is this review happening?

I'm being shown it in one of the books. It's almost like a little video inside the book that plays back certain scenes.

Well just tell me the scenes that are played back and the discussions you have with Inka.

I get the scene running up to my death. I'd given up on life, given up on learning. He is asking how things could have been different.

And what do you say?

I could have been more active, more outgoing. I could have not felt sorry for myself. I had the option to live more in the present, but at that stage I was looking more to the future and dying. It brings the sadness back. Then he flips back. There were some opportunities that I had after my husband's death that I didn't take up. I could have listened to certain people's advice. I could have taken a different path and that would've helped me to not be so sad in my later years.

What is it that stopped you from recognizing this advice?

I was too caught up in the grief of losing my husband. I just wanted to believe that I just had to wait until I joined him. I didn't want to believe that I still had a life to live.

Does your spirit guide offer any advice at this point?

He's saying that it was quite a normal human emotion to feel as I did, but he feels that I took it too far.

And at a soul level, what do you think?

I agree.

Are there any other scenes that you review in this book?

We go back to some happier times when our children were young, and how we both did a lot of work educating them, and trying to instill values of self worth and confidence.

And what does Inka say about that?

He's praising me for the work that I did with the children, and how it's helped them have a good start in their lives. He's showing me other scenes where I've done it with other people. That's one of my skills, he says.

At the end of this review Liz is also reminded of a minor incident. This provides an important reminder for us all that we are all connected as part of the ultimate Source:

> He says I could have been nicer to a certain person that I just didn't like, and there was no real reason for it. He's showing me how we're all connected.

This is also one of the few cases where a subject has a review with both their guide and their elders. We will return to find out more about Liz's situation shortly.

The final case of life review comes from Liam Thompson, who experiences it in two parts. The first commences early, during transition and before healing. It covers his suicide in his last life that renders this such an interesting case, because a number of the pioneers agree that this seems to be the one act that is looked on unfavorably even in the light realms. He reports immediately on leaving his body that he meets his spirit guide who is 'shaking his head in disgust'. His concern seems even more justified when we now find that this is part of a repeating pattern that has continued into his current life:

I need to go and discuss what's happened. Again. I always do this.
Do you know who it is you're going to be meeting?
My spirit guide. He's standing with his arms crossed, shaking his head. I'm like the little pupil and he's the teacher. He's got a long beard and a long white gown. He's full of love and warmth, but at the same time he's strict. He's been my guide for a number of lives now.
Does he talk to you telepathically?
Yes. Well, it's more than telepathy, it's feelings as well, it's everything. I can see inside his mind and he can see inside mine. Except he can keep certain things from me. I'm still learning how to do that.
Tell me what happens in this review.
He's asking me why I always take the easy way out. I have a problem with facing problems.
What do you say?
I don't get angry, but he needs to understand that I need an easier life now. I'm sick of doing these really hard ones.
Is he giving you any advice?
He tells me I need to stop thinking about things so much. I need to just learn to live, instead of being so introverted. I need to experience the world around me, rather than just experiencing the world within me. I'm my own worst enemy. Whatever I feel inside me, I project onto the world around. Most situations aren't as bad as they seem, but I seem to make them harder.
Does your guide say anything else to you at this point?

He knows I need to have a rest for a bit.

What about you committing suicide, does he have anything to say about that?

In the last couple of lives I've done exactly the same thing, so he doesn't want to repeat himself.

Is your guide projecting information to you about those lives right now, to help you understand the patterns?

Yes, and he's projecting love as well.

Ask him to review those two previous lives where you've ended up committing suicide.

[Whispers to himself] I can't say any more, because I'm in the same situation right now in this [current] life as well. I need to learn for myself.

Suicide is apparently one of the worst situations we can face in the light realms unless it relates to serious illness. However this account is hardly a serious judgment from on high. Despite his frankness, his spirit guide is still loving and caring, and also anxious to help. It is also interesting that his recall of some of the details of this original discussion is blocked because he is facing the same situation in his current life.

The second element of Liam's review is a more formal session that comes after his healing and initial reunion with his soul group, during which he too looks at his life book. In this interlife he calls it 'halls of learning' rather than a library. Here it becomes even clearer that his guide is blocking certain important information from his conscious mind:

I'm in the halls, learning, studying, looking at the life books. I'm with my guide, and I need to discuss things in more detail.

Just have a look around you, and tell me what this place is like.

It's Grecian, with marble pillars. It's vast, ginormous! And it twinkles.

What are you doing in this place?

I'm sat down at a table. My guide's facing me. We're going over the events that led to me being self-destructive in my last life, and connecting them to previous lives as well.

Can you give me some more details?

I can't. As I said earlier, it's because I'm in the same situation in this life. I've got to work things out for myself.

Ok, and then what happens next?

I know we worked out a solution at the time. There's always a solution, but right now I don't know what it is.

The key point here is that Liam and his guide obviously did try to work out a solution to his suicide problem during his last interlife, even though in revisiting it he is not allowed to know exactly what that solution was. This makes sense because the subjects talk about their lives in terms of 'learning'. As we will see plans are made during the interlife to maximize this. These plans are not remembered consciously while incarnate, because to do so would massively reduce the learning potential. It is only by tackling various situations in our life with complete free will, that we make the experiences useful.

Reviews with the Elders

The majority of the pioneers report that at some point during the interlife their clients meet with groups of spirits that had evolved beyond the need to incarnate. The names they use are the 'Council' or 'Elders'. The subjects referred to these names, but also called them the 'Higher Ones', 'Wise Ones' or 'Masters of Light'. There is no consistent name used in the interlife, so for convenience they have all been referred to as 'elders' in the narrative. The elders are consistently described as being kind and loving, and not as sitting in judgment.

Only two of the subjects do not mention their elders at all, in either the review or planning context. For those that have a past life review with the elders the spirit guide is present, although often they are relatively inactive as an observer. Their presence is understandable because the guide will have been involved with the previous planning for that life. However it must be remembered that this was a sample size of 15. Generally more experienced souls need less support from the guide than younger ones. Indeed, some experienced souls do not need the presence of their guide at all. As we have come to expect, these meetings are perceived in surroundings in whatever form the soul chooses.

Wendy Simpson, one of the subjects with no prior knowledge of interlife, describes the meeting with her elders. We will recall her previous past life as the old man in the desert with a tunnel experience following death. This review is unusual in that she meets them immediately after her transition, even before she has received any healing:

It's like I'm being guided. There's some sort of learning to be done. I am in the presence of three light beings.
Do you have a name for them?
I get the feeling they are 'masters of light'.
What is communicated to you?
They feel very loving. It's like they are showing me the lessons and experiences of what that lifetime was about.
What were they?
Hardship, and not understanding people, the way I treated the people I came into contact with. I must be more understanding and loving.

She is asked if this is part of any sort of pattern, and her elders reveal that she has had several past lives working on the same theme of how she treats other people:

The first one seems to be a poor woman, again I think she's in a desert area, and she's quite plump. I get the sense that she is greedy and protective. There are two children with her. She has had to fight for everything, and she is very poor.

How is that life related?

I think it's the way she treats people. She feels a bit aggressive.

What about the next life?

It's a different part of the world. Spain. She is also a big lady, with a dark cloth on her head, made of wool. She's got lots of children around her, and I can hear her shouting a lot. She's good with children, but she keeps herself with her family and doesn't meet other people so much.

How does that relate to the theme you've been working on?

There's a fair bit of aggression in her, and she's kind of materialistic towards her family. It's also about the way she communicates, and again how she treats others. She is too cool and distant.

We might recall that Jack Hammond's problem during his life as a young WW2 soldier, which was initially revealed by his welcoming party playing a joke on him by cloaking themselves, had something to do with his ego. When he meets with his elders we find that he too has a repetitive problem with how he treats others. This has occurred in previous lives and he is supposed to be working on it in this life too:

There's three people behind a desk, and I'm sitting in front of them. I feel ok. It's serious, but there's no sternness. It's like I'm having to give an account of myself, but not as I'd experience it on earth. This is benign. I guess I'm being reviewed... I feel that there were things I could have done in that life, even though it was short. There were opportunities, and I never took them... To be more giving of myself, more loving, a nicer person. I'm sensing that, for want of a better word, there's disapproval because I did have opportunities and I did what I've done before in other lives. Disapprove is probably too strong a word though... It's like a double-whammy. When I helped my friend at the time of my death I showed the giving of oneself that I should have done with the opportunities before that. I think I was quite a loner, quite a solitary person in my twenty-odd years. I was supposed to be learning to be more giving, but it didn't happen until right at the very end... In this life I need to continue to learn to love, to not be so aloof, to give. It's like if I want this contact, this closeness, I have to give it first. It's like I expect to receive it without having to give it in return.

By contrast Liz Kendry meets with her elders straight after her preparatory review with her guide that was discussed previously. Her spirit guide Inka joins her, but instead of being an observer the guide helps her by communicating about the past life to the elders. The elders remind her that this is not the first time she has given up on life after the death of her husband:

I have to go see the elders. Inka leads the way and he's going to give a summary to them.

Before you start that, just describe the place that you find yourself in.

It's kind of a circular room, with a domed roof and sort of white walls. There's some sort of a raised cross on the floor, which looks like it's made of marble. In fact it's a little step up that goes across the whole room.

How many spirits of light can you see?

Six... They're sat down. There seems to be a focus on just one, the rest are not going to be speaking.

Ok, and describe that one.

He has white hair, a white beard, a white gown. Bright blue eyes, and kind of a rounded shape nose. He's got a very kind face, and he's trying to make me feel at ease. I'm worried because in the last decade or so of my life I was just not living, I was wasting life and it's happened before.

How many times has this happened before?
Three.

Is it the same kind of thing where you've had an attachment to a loved one?
Yes, it's always my husband dying, and then I feel there's no life to live afterwards.

What does this spirit of light say to you?
He says they're going to give me more help next time. They will let it be known to me, through other people or my own consciousness that we don't die when our bodies die, so I won't feel that loss as I have in previous lives.

Probably the most detailed and revealing elder review comes from Laura Harper. She is with her guide Iscanara, and it commences with some interesting details of the atmosphere:

Describe where you go to with Iscanara.
She takes me to see the council of wise ones. We're approaching a round temple made of golden yellow stone, with a door.

Do you go inside this temple?
Yes, and there's a long, very narrow corridor, which opens out into this big round room.

Tell me what you can see?
It has a domed ceiling that looks as if it's made from thin, light-permeable shell. I can see three wise ones. They're dressed in velvet cloaks of the deepest sort of blue-purple, with gold trimming.

Is Iscanara with you?

She's stepped back. She's behind me.

Does one of these figures address you?

They [laughs] look as if they've been to a party actually, they look, um, sort of comical.

Just describe the facial expressions on the one that stands out.

The one in the middle has got these incredibly crinkly, smiley eyes. They have almost disappeared into his smile.

Tell me what happens.

It feels as if this room is just alive with laughter. I'm just being told to 'lie back in the laughter'. I think I expected to come in here and it to be like some sort of exalted holy place, but it's just full of laughter and mischief and a kind of golden knowing. It's joyfulness. It's grace, the very stuff of existence. It's being. It's loving. It's love, really.

She is asked here why they are choosing to show her such a joyous atmosphere:

Because I take myself so seriously. I'm even trying to take myself seriously in here… The sense I get is that it's very honorable to be diligent and serious, but not necessary. It's necessary to be light. To be a light being, working in light. To take myself lightly. They have a message for me about hatred as well. They say it's an intense light charge, with the wrong interpretation. By labeling it as hatred, it becomes a weapon, like a sword, double-edged. They're telling me to expand so that my being can experience it as joy.

This discussion of turning negative emotions into joy is perhaps something we can all consider. She then continues with the elders in the library environment, where she is helped to see the cause of her hatred in the context of a number of previous lives:

They take down this volume. One image that I'm seeing at the moment is a sort of phalanx, like marching centurions. They're marching warrior men with close fitting metal helmets, and what I'm seeing is just being ground underfoot mercilessly. As women with no defense we are just ground under foot by this moving machine of willful warrior men... There are children as well. They're also ground underfoot. ... My heart could experience it as love and grief for my children and all the others, you know? To narrow it down to hatred binds me to that. If you stay tight like a sharp point, then the hatred is in the point and it's a weapon. If you stay loose and expand, then the heart is dealing with the faces of love... I'm being shown that fighting back has no purpose. It remains like a razor that wants blood.... I think it feels as if the message is just to expand, in the middle, in my heart, to just open. Open. Open. Open. It's almost like the blow just passes straight through you then. Open. Stay open and then it's a touch of joy.

Laura had indicated before the session that she wanted to understand more about a problem in her current life. These are worrying thoughts of being attacked and feelings of fear and shame when talking to small groups:

Yes. They say it is the same, but it's a different life memory involving the fear and shame of being stoned to death. This is essentially the same as the boots of the soldiers that crushed us underfoot. It's the same impact. It's the same meeting of a hard, unresisting, attacking, force... So it's all about surrender, about letting go of resistance. What they're actually showing me is that even the most brutal attack can be experienced as a caress of love. Every knife, every bullet, every weapon, every bomb. That it's my ego that wants to meddle with another soul's journey, by taking it as an attack. My own soul path is about learning, surrender, and emptying. Every weapon that seems to harm is the perpetrator's journey, and it's only my wanting to meddle in that other person's journey that makes it an injury and a wound. If I want to meddle in that other person's journey, then I'm going to receive it as 'you've done me wrong'.

Continuing this she is asked if the past life she has just experienced before the interlife as an old man watching his town being invaded is also related to all this in some way:

Yes it is, because I could have meddled instead of surrendering at the time. It can seem quite passive, like opting out. If I had meddled in the affairs of the people, because my strength had gone, I would have fouled it up... Actually, when the people came up the hill and stayed briefly under my wings, we were able to receive something of a stillness and a surrender. It's love really, it's love that would have strengthened them for whatever was to follow. So it is the same in a way. I can see that I've puffed myself up in the past and felt like 'How dare somebody throw me a left hook from outside. How dare they. I must prove to them how bad they are', but it's meddling.

This most insightful session concludes with some advice from another of Laura's elders, who she perceives as a woman:

She says 'be soft'. When you surrender and become empty, you become a much clearer conductor of the light. If we are always emptier we can conduct a greater charge, without any impedance. They're showing me that even a canon ball can go straight through my chest and not harm me at all if I stay light. If it takes my life force away I have the opportunity to reform and come back in another time and place.

In summary, while the more experienced souls may review the past life unaided, more frequently it involves the presence of the spirit guide or elders. Their role is to assist in understanding the past life. As Nadine Castelle commented, 'My guide is with me... to help me if I need help, but I know if there is something I should have done that didn't match my original intentions'. Often we can be our own worst critic and need to be reminded of the accomplishments as Liz Kendry reported, 'He's praising me for the work I did... showing me other scenes... that's one of my skills he says'. Any areas not achieved sets the basis for the next life plan as Jack Hammond was quick to conclude, 'I was supposed to learn not to be so aloof but it did not happen until the very end... I need to continue to learn'.

Knowledge of the past life and its review brings an understanding of the themes and lessons to a person's conscious mind. Often these are aspects not completely grasped in the current life. When accepted and integrated, it brings a greater prospect of healing and spiritual growth.

4

SOUL GROUPS

Be a well baked loaf and lord of the table.
Come and be served to your brothers.
You have been a source of pain,
now you'll be the delight.
Jelaluddin Rumi, Sufi mystic, 13th Century.

The idea that we all have soul mates and share a special bond with them over many lives has received widespread attention in recent decades. The interlife pioneers universally acknowledge this, particularly that all souls seem to belong to a close-knit soul group. Virtually all the subjects confirmed this, with only one who did not describe the experience. This of course does not mean that the subject was without a soul group. There may simply have been no activity with the soul group in that interlife, or that the experience was of no great importance.

The spread of the number of souls in the group reported by the subjects is summarized in the following table:

No. Souls	No.	Subjects
1 to 5	2	15%
6 to 10	5	38%
11 to 15	4	31%
16 to 20	1	8%
21 to 30	1	8%

In order to maximize the therapeutic benefit of an interlife, clients are normally asked which soul group members they recognize in the past life and also their current life. This was also applied to the subjects who recognized them with or without prompting. On occasions it was extended into asking about soul mates they had not yet met in their current life but would in the future. Sometimes this information was forthcoming but sometimes it was blocked. To find out too much information at a conscious level could affect the freewill of the subject.

The soul mates recognized by the subjects came from family members such as grandparents, parents, siblings or children. On other occasions they were recognized as friends and other acquaintances. Their roles and relationships with the subject would often change from one life to the next. Sometimes they were there for support and help and on other occasions they played the role of perpetrator to bring about some learning. The inclusions or omissions from the composition of the soul group were often a surprise for the subject. For example, long-term partners or spouses and close family members were not always close soul mates.

One specific aspect of soul group activity involves joint planning for the next life and will be covered later. Here the focus is on the more general nature and activities of soul groups and their member's interactions.

Soul Mates

The reunion with the soul mates usually occurs after healing, and either before or after some sort of life review. However we have already seen that Jack Hammond was met by his six soul mates on transition, and after his elder review he returns to his group to learn more about his aloofness and the joke they played on him. This time he recognizes people from his previous life as a young soldier:

I want to go off and be alone just to contemplate, but I'm being urged, and I feel Garth's got something to do with this, to go and be with people. Not to be this aloof, alone person. Ah, I see, to go back to see the others. That's what it's all about, that's what their joke's about. They appeared to be mysterious and aloof. Everybody's having a good old crack at me, trying to teach me this lesson... It's like they're saying 'see, do you get it?' and 'come and be with us, come and be giving'. I'm having my turn as well. I'm pointing out to my mum and dad that they could have helped, they could have been more giving. The same goes for one or two of the others as well... It seems to be quite a major thing in this group. We've got a major job on, to do with opening up and giving, and not just expecting it. Learning to just let go, and it will happen. One way or another, we all struggle with that, with the possible exception of my grandmother. She seems to be such a lovely, benign being. Almost like she's the matriarch saying 'come on children, we'll all roll with this', like she's a graduate already... When I say they have a crack at me and I have a crack at them, there's not a hint of malice or anything. It's like you can get out this thought or get out those words and it's both given and accepted with love. It's like 'yeah, yeah, ok'.

This latter observation of Jack's is important. On occasions when souls reunite with their group there are difficult issues from the most recent life that need to be shared and discussed. What is clear is that total honesty is always accompanied by unlimited love, just as with the guide or elder review. There is no real sense of harshness or criticism, and certainly not of judgment. We have seen that Lisbet Halvorsen was less than happy about the life she had just led as a slave trader, and she too makes this point well:

I recognize my soul group, we understand each other. Usually when we come back it's happy and light, but this time it feels serious because of the life I've just led. But they are still welcoming me with love and compassion.

Most souls report that reuniting with their soul group is nothing more than pure bliss, and that every effort is made to welcome the departed soul back. In fact Nadine Castelle specifically mentions during the latter stages of her interlife experience that she has to return to her group because they are 'throwing a celebration for someone who has just come back'. Despite her minimal prior knowledge, Veronica Perry in her first session provides an excellent unprompted account of her joy in being reunited with her 20 soul mates. Of these she recognizes 15 from her current life:

I'm going to see my group... I'm so pleased to see them all. We're all really happy to see each other... There's so much happiness and love and it feels like there's fun and laughter and joy and love. It's just overwhelming... There's lots of banter. We're all greeting each other and we just know what each other is thinking... It's like we're all catching up with what we're all doing, and it only takes a split second for all those thoughts and images to come through.

In the same theme, while Liz Kendry is delighted to be reunited with her six soul mates, she is particularly relieved to be reunited with the husband who had died before her in her last life:

I feel their love and their warmth and their energy wrapping around mine. They're all happy to see me... It's very comforting. I realize I haven't let go of my husband, it's like we're holding hands the whole time... I just don't want to let go of him.

In fact this same soul has played the role of her husband in each of the lives in which she had faced the problem of giving up after his death.

This rare example of two souls adopting the same relationship over a number of lives is probably the closest we can get to the idea that we can have an extra-special soul mate, perhaps even a 'twin-soul'. As enticing as this idea might sound, it only seems to happen when there is a repetitive problem to work on. The more experienced souls tend to work with all their soul group and sometimes members from other groups.

After this initial reunion Liz goes off for the past-life review before rejoining her soul group. At this point she reports that 'we talk about our last lives, and compare notes on who did what and how we could have improved'. When Lisbet Halvorsen returns to her soul group later in her session, she describes how they 'discuss important things, what we have done and what we will do, we make plans', while Katja Eisler informs us that her group 'shares information about difficulties in physical lives'. So it is clear that this sort of discussion forms the main basis of soul group interaction after the pure bliss and excitement of the initial reunion has subsided.

Magnus Bergen is another subject with no prior knowledge who meets with his group and raises an interesting new aspect, that of members of the group who are absent:

It's like I meet some people I knew from before, a group of souls.
How many are there?
I'll have to ask them to line up [pause while counting]. 13 or 15, but they're not all here.
How do you know they are missing?
I just know.
What does it feel like to be with them?
I feel very much at home here. They have smiles on their faces. It's just good to be here, with nothing expected of you, and nothing wrong.

Liam Thompson's account of meeting up with the seven other members of his soul group is excellent, and he provides further details about absent friends:

> I'm going to meet my group.
> *How many can you count?*
> Seven.
> *And how are they showing themselves to you?*
> As energy.
> *Just have a look at their colors, and tell me what they are?*
> They're like white with blue. They're all ahead of me.
> *What does it feel like?*
> Coming home. Glad to be back. We all come together and it's like a hug of energy all around. They're all pleased to see me, and I'm very pleased to see all of them. There's one that is still living.
> *Is he not joining in on this hug?*
> No. He's only left a small amount of energy, and that is really dormant. You can't really do anything with that.

To pick up on this issue of souls who are incarnate, Newton suggests that in the light realms these souls tend to be perceived by their fellows as relatively dormant. Here Liam introduces the important point that this is only the case if they have taken the bulk of their soul energy with them. Those that leave a significant portion behind in the light realms can remain quite active. This enables subjects to regularly recognize and interact with soul mates who are still incarnate in this life during the interlife session. Continuing with Liam:

> *Go through them one by one and tell me if you see any that you recognize.*
> There's one that I recognize, two that I recognize.
> *Tell me their names.*

Jamie, and my mum in this life are here as well. She's normally my mum. She's very mother-like and caring.

Is there anyone else that you recognize?

Rose. Hmm.

Is Rose in incarnation at the moment?

Yes.

Is she able to communicate to you about any work you may do together?

No. We haven't met yet.

He realizes that one is Rose, the girl he fell in love with in Ireland in his past life. She refused to run away with him and this contributed to him killing himself. When asked whether she can reveal anything about a possible role in his current life, once again his blocks seem to come into play when he replies 'no, we haven't met yet'. By contrast when Lene Haugland meets up with her soul group in the next chapter, she is given a small amount of information about people she has yet to meet in this life. All of them will apparently be in other parts of the world.

Soul Experience

Liam continues by describing the deftness of touch his soul mates display towards his repetitive problem of taking his own life:

They're teasing me. They're all very light-hearted because I've done it again. They say it's becoming repetitive, but at the same time their taunts are serious as well. They know that I need to catch up with them and they don't want me to fall behind.

If you don't catch up with them, what will that mean?

I'll have to go into another group

What aspect are you currently working on?

I'm working on myself. My self-esteem, self-confidence. I need to realize that I'm the most important person in my life. I need to obtain some self-love.

Liam's report that he might 'fall behind' the other members of his group raises an important point about the level of soul experience. The members of any soul group tend to be at a similar level. So it follows that different groups will be at various levels based on factors such as the number of lives they will have had. Because all souls will learn specific lessons faster or slower than others there may come a point when a soul needs to leave the group to go to another.

The type of incarnate life a person lives is no indication of their level of development. Sometimes the most experienced souls can choose the most apparently difficult and impoverished lives deliberately. Newton identified the color of soul energy to highlight a grading system from 'beginner', to 'advanced' souls. Grayish for younger souls through a range of colors including yellow, orange and greens to purple for the more developed ones. This knowledge can be used to identify soul group members in an interlife because they will have similar energy colors. Liam confirms this when he meets his soul group and they all have the energy colors of 'white with blue'.

Asking for the soul color to establish the advancement of the soul is not something that I or many other interlife therapists are particularly keen to emphasize. This is because it may introduce a spiritual elitism from the clients. It may also represent something of an oversimplification. For example Magnus Bergen with no prior interlife knowledge makes an interesting observation when he reports that the predominantly yellow and green colors he perceives in his core during healing represent 'the experiences that I have with me'. Then, when asked why this color has changed when he is with his soul group, he responds: 'It's not my soul that's blue, this is just the shape that we all have when I'm together with these other souls.' It seems that at least on some occasions these colors may represent emotions and states of mind that can change depending on the circumstances, rather than always a level of development.

Group Dynamics

Soul groups tend to have a theme on which all the members are working together. For example, we have seen that Jack Hammond's group have a 'major job on, to do with opening up and giving' and this appears to be what can be referred to as an emotional lesson. On the other hand, the theme can also be the development of a specialist skill such as healing. Whatever the theme it appears that soul groups are periodically disbanded when the majority of their members are ready to move onto other areas.

Some of the subjects were asked to provide information on the number of lifetimes they had been with their current soul group. Typically this ranged from very few because the group was relatively new, through to as many as nearly one hundred. Despite his lack of prior knowledge Magnus Bergen again provided an intriguing response: 'I am getting 17, but I'm not sure what to describe as lifetimes because they're not always reincarnations. We do other work too.' Magnus appears to be referring to the option that some souls have of developing in the spirit realms rather than through a physical incarnation. Generally this is a slower process because in physical form emotions can be fully experienced and these play such an important role in soul development.

Marta Petersen provides some interesting details about changing soul groups. We saw in the previous chapter that, in her last life as a young girl in WW2 Warsaw, she was assisting her mother with 'harmonizing her energy'. We join her as she is discussing the theme of her soul group:

It's harmonizing energy.
How many lifetimes have you been with this group?

Eighty-four.

Have all the lifetimes been about harmonizing?

Yes. Of course I've had additional lessons as well. I was in a different group before this.

What was the theme of that group?

Also something to do with energy, I worked a lot with mysticism.

How did you know it was time to leave that group?

We all split up and we had to specialize in another thing.

Was this your choice?

It was our choice, we felt it was time we went in different directions.

Another interesting area of group dynamics is the extent to which souls work with members of other soul groups. Given the size of even the larger soul groups relative to the number of people we meet in life, it is hardly surprising that we sometimes make detailed plans for incarnate interaction with others from outside of our immediate group. We will find later that a number of our subjects report that they do exactly this, with Lisbet Halvorsen in particular discussing the idea of broader planning interactions in some detail. She also reports that none of her immediate soul group of four were with her either in her past or her current life, and that instead the people she recognizes come from a broader group of souls for whom she acts as a teacher. To some extent all this confirms Newton's suggestion of larger, secondary groups of souls who work together less closely or frequently. However, despite the prior exposure that some of them had to his work, none of our subjects explicitly mentions a well-defined secondary grouping, and this suggests that there is probably a high degree of fluidity in this process.

The work with souls from other groups is not just limited to incarnating together. Nadine Castelle provides an interesting example of how souls can share their knowledge more broadly while in the light realms:

> I'm with two others from another soul group. We're relating to each other what we would like to do next, because we all have the same objectives, and we just want to share our knowledge... One of them has the choice to go into the medical profession in their next life, and I tell them my experience, and they are just absorbing the energy information that I took with me so that they can better prepare for what they need to do. The other one is sharing what they will be doing in their next lifetime, their choice in some kind of structural art, to do with energy forms in art and the feeling of heat and resonance from particular matter.

Spirit Guides

We have already gained a pretty reasonable impression of the nature of spirit guides, but some further aspects are worth considering. First, four of the subjects did not describe meeting any sort of guide figure. This does not necessary mean they have not got one. Merely that aspect of their interlife experience was of no great importance to them, or that there was no meeting. Second, spirit guides in the light realms can show themselves in their normal energy form or human form. All 11 subjects who met with their spirit guide perceived them having some human form, with 8 sensing a male form and 3 female.

Another aspect is the relationship between soul groups and spirit guides. Newton is the only person to discuss this aspect in any great depth. He suggests that the members of any given soul group share the same guide. Whilst there is insufficient information with the subjects to confirm this, sometimes I have found that it is not always the case. However, the intriguing question is what happens when a soul changes soul group? Marta Petersen continues her report of changing from her current soul group to a new one being offered to her:

I was in a different group before this. We all split up and we had to specialize in another thing.

Was this your choice?

Yes, we felt it was time we went in different directions.

Do you keep the same spirit guide?

No, I had a different guide at the time.

How did you choose your spirit guide?

I had different choices in the different groups but I felt like this group and this guide would suit me very well.

So do the guide and group go together?

No, but this group and this special guide were presented to me as a combined choice.

A complexity arising out of the research is the possibility that especially more experienced souls might have more than one guide, just as they might work with more than one group. Veronica Perry's first session has her apparently met by multiple guides and helpers.

I can see seven beautiful lights coming towards me.... It's my spirit guides come to collect me... I've had other spirits of light helping me with different things. There is a group that oversees your choices, and your lives, and your learning, and some are drawn to guide you in different experiences, or you're drawn to them.

Her healing is assisted by two 'very different characters', one a 'playful' guide and the other a rather more remote figure that she describes as a 'teacher'. She also hints that she also approaches other guides when needed. It appears that the allocation of spirit guides may be more fluid that previously suggested.

5

SPECIALIST ACTIVITIES

One instant is eternity.
Eternity is the now.
When you see through this one instant,
you see through the one who sees.
Wu-Men, Chinese Zen Master, 13th Century.

The chapter on reviewing past lives highlighted the emotional lessons that the subjects were learning. Laura was working on 'hatred and fear', Liz on 'not giving up on life following the death of a loved one'. Lisbeth was working on 'not being in connection with her feelings', Nadine on 'dealing with negative energy' and Liam on his repetitive suicides. The last chapter on soul groups introduced the idea that soul groups have an emotional theme that all members are learning. Jack's group was working on 'opening up and giving', Marta's group on 'harmonizing energy'. Now we are moving to a further theme that some souls groups have which is learning a specialist skill.

Healers, Guides and Teachers
We have already reviewed David Stephens's detailed description of training to be a healer in the light realms. Now we move to Lisbet Halvorsen, who uses her past life as a slave trader to teach other souls about her experience. This suggests that it may not have been such a waste of life after all:

There's like a panel and I'm standing in the middle, and it's like I'm lecturing…The room is in energy form, but it looks like an auditorium, sort of a half-circle that is almost closed... It's packed with maybe a hundred people in ten rows... I'm talking about how easy it is to make mistakes, using my last life as an example... I show them pictures from that life and they get to feel what it was like, they get to feel the other people's pain, and they get to feel what it was like to be me with no connection to my feelings... It's like I show them on a big screen, I think about it and they see it. It's a good way of learning... We're hoping that they will remember... This is my way of teaching, to share my experience... There was a panel of three or four above me who told me this was a way I could do it... Now they are splitting into small groups, and talking about it and doing exercises, looking at different lives and possible opportunities and solutions, and I'm just walking around helping them.

Although this illustrates Lisbet's specialist work as a teacher, it is also a wonderful example of the ongoing classroom learning that most of the pioneers mention. It confirms the idea previously discussed that souls are able to put themselves in the position of those they have hurt. Learning can go far further than the mere replaying of events of a past life as they happened. It can extend to examining the other's life as well and feeling the other person's pain. There is also the suggestion that souls can role-play alternative courses of action to see what the effects would have been. This demonstrates the extent of the assistance available to us in the light realms when we are attempting to learn and grow.

Marta Petersen is another subject who takes the role of teacher. After her own life review in the library of life books, she perceives herself moving down a hall to a classroom. Notice also how she corrects me quite abruptly when I mistakenly assume that she is a pupil. This just serves to remind us of the extent to which subjects are in charge of their own interlife experience rather than being blindly led by the therapist:

I go to another classroom. Someone there is expecting me.

Just describe what it is like.

It's just down the hall. It looks like a regular classroom, with tables and a blackboard. There are no books though.

How many students are there?

Eight.

And what is this class about?

I like to work by talking about an experience I have had in one of my lives, and discussing it with the students. Then they give their view of what they would have done in that situation, and we talk about choices and so on.

Are you being taught any specific subject?

No, I'm the teacher.

Oh. So what are you teaching?

How to keep their energy level. How to not let other people steal their energy from them when they are incarnate. How to become more aware of your own energy and the energy of others, and not letting people take it from you, or not taking it from them.

How do people take energy from others?

With negative thoughts and fear.

How do you teach this?

First of all they have to become aware of their own energy, because if they don't feel it they can't protect it. On earth you need to become aware of your body and what it does, how it reacts when you get insecure, and whether you can control it when someone comes up to you with negative feelings and emotions. So they have to become aware of the whole energy within their body.

And how can someone tune into their own energy?

By acting on impulses. It is the biggest thing we forget when we are on earth. We ignore our impulses. Some call it intuition.

How do you know when it is time to finish this lesson?

They can only absorb a limited amount of information, so this is only one of many lessons. This is something they are going to learn in many lives to come, and I will repeat my lesson whenever it is needed between their lives, as a reminder.

Marta's remarks indicate that she and perhaps her soul mates are in training to be guides as well. The narrative now switches to the question of how she was able to find herself on the same train going to the concentration camp as her parents. This enables her to die with her mother as planned, despite her previous decision to hide when the Germans took her parents away:

Ask your guide how he managed to arrange for you to find your mum again.

There were a number of choices. I could have died before I met up with her on the train, but the whole point was for me to die with her. So it was arranged that even if the soldiers didn't pick me up initially, I would still end up on the same train as she was.

Ask your spirit guide how they manage to get people to do things so that the outcome is what they want.

They can push people, give them ideas, and encourage them to go in a certain direction.

While they are asleep?

Even while they are awake. He is very powerful. I have tried to do this myself before. We can practice on people while they sleep, and it's very funny. We do it regularly to keep up the training.

And how does this work, sending your ideas down to people?

We have to concentrate a lot, and often there are two or three of us. Dreams are the easiest way.

Do you have to have an energy link to these people?

The people we practice on are pointed out to us, because we can't just choose a random person who is asleep. So someone else sees to it that there is a contact, or they mentally point out the person we can practice on, because we don't want to harm anyone or scare them. As long as it's harmless it's fine, and usually it's not someone we know.

This idea of experienced souls being able to influence people in the physical realm via their dreams is fairly widely reported. However to do it while we are awake would presumably involve the planting of a strong intuition or a sudden coincidence that we would be unlikely to ignore. All of this is clearly related to the way in which we ourselves attempt to stick to our life plan, sometimes in conjunction with our souls mates and others. How we achieve this will be picked up later.

Intellectual Pursuits

Whitton is the only pioneer who makes a brief reference to what can be called intellectual studies in 'vast halls of learning equipped with libraries and seminar rooms'. Within them 'doctors and lawyers study their respective disciplines, while others apply themselves to such subjects as the laws of the universe and other metaphysical topics'. This is clearly not the same setting as the library of life books, which seems to be more oriented towards emotional lessons.

Lene Haugland is our one subject who confirms such pursuit of intellectual skills, fortunately in great detail. She is also unusual in that she finds herself so engaged in this at a very early stage, immediately after her transition and initial healing. The 'classroom' she describes is equipped with some sort of screen and books that can come alive like a movie. This is not dissimilar to life books, but the nature of the information within them is clearly very different:

I see this big, big room. It's like a classroom in a way, and it looks like it could be from the old days, a hundred odd years ago... I see big wooden tables and chairs, and the walls are also wooden. It's not light, it's quite dark. There's a lot of books in here, big books, and people are reading and writing in them. At the end of the room is like a screen.

Are there any other presences in this room?

Yes, there's a lot of people.

How are they showing themselves to you?

In human form but everybody here has long, white, shiny hair. No one is talking to each other, they are only concerned with the books. They are carrying them around, writing in them, reading from them. In front of the screen is a machine, and it's like the screen is three-dimensional. It's deep, deep, deep, deep.

Have you ever been here before?

Yes.

And what do you use the screen for?

I can step into it if I want. I have this feeling that I could disappear. It's another way of going deeper, it's like I'm going to another place.

So what are you doing here this time?

I think I've worked in here with the books before. When I open one, it's not like a real book, it's as if there's a movie inside it. As if it's alive.

Do these books have different titles?

Yes.

What's the title of the one you're looking at?

'Keys'.

And what are you reading about?

It's hard to see. I get this feeling it's got something to do with technological things, like time and space. It's spinning so fast.

Just have a look at one of the pages and tell me the information that's there.

I see this circle, and it's like an eclipse followed by a full moon.

It's dark, then it's glowing then it's lights, but I don't know what this means.

What is it that's drawn you to look at this book?

The word that comes to me is astronomy and geometry. It's important for me to know some connection lines between planets and solar systems. It's as if I carry some information about some sort of connection.

Do you use any other books in the library?

The person on the next table has this book about flowers, fantastic flowers. I've never seen those kinds of flowers before. It's only these special people that work here. They have this long, shiny hair, they are quite small, and they have got quite big noses.

Do they have some special name, or job?

They are not just librarians, it seems like it's their job to read the books, but they only read the ones they need. The first person I saw, his name is Marly, and I think he has the special job of meeting people when they come in.

Can any soul come to this library?

No. You need to have a connection. I don't know why I'm allowed in here because I'm not one of them, but I have been allowed to be here for some reason.

Lene then finds herself moving through a hallway into another room where souls rather than studying seem to be engaged in a more automatic form of information acquisition:

Ok, tell me what you do next.

I'm in a kind of classroom, with benches but no tables.

And how many people are there?

I'll count. [Whispers] One, two, three, there are five people. They are not sitting together and talking to each other, it's like they are absorbing something, a kind of energy. It seems like a kind of loading station. It's for some kind of information, and if they are sitting in different places they are getting different information.

Are you going to sit down and get some information at this place?

No, no. I'm just passing through.

Have you ever used this place yourself for loading information?

Yes.

Does this have the same type of information as the library you went to?

It's the same kind of information, but they are not taking it in through the eyes. The library was more physical and mental. In this place you just sit there and absorb.

When she then moves on to reunite with her soul group we find that their theme involves working and communicating with timeless pictorial symbols with a mathematical underpinning:

What's the current purpose of this soul group?

We're working with symbols. We communicate with them, because we get more exact information that way.

Is this unique to your group?

No, it is something that has been used by many soul groups. Everybody who uses them knows what the symbols mean, they are like pictures, a language of mathematics.

Is it possible for this information to be written down on earth?

Yes it is, but what makes them so hard to use in the way we did before, long ago, is that different people and cultures have been giving them different names and meanings, so the original meanings are not clear any more.

Here Lene appears to be describing some sort of archetypal 'language of the universe', and it is interesting that she reports that it was in common use on earth at one time, but has now been so distorted by different cultures that its original meaning has become obscured.

Working with Energy

Newton provides a number of examples of subjects working creatively with energy. Several of the subjects confirm this idea, to such an extent that the basic work of energy manipulation may be not so much a specialism as something that all souls engage in to some extent.

A fine example of this comes from Liam Thompson on his second meeting with his soul group:

What is happening with your soul group now?
They're creating with their energy. They're all healers and I am as well. They're making forms, shapes.
And what are these shapes?
Pure energy.
Whereabouts do they get this energy from?
I think they channel it from the source.
What are they doing with this energy?
Hmm. Learning how to create solid matter. Working on small things at first. I'm not sure how to do it exactly... stones...Clear, focused thoughts.
Does this take a lot of practice?
Yes. It takes a lot of practice. It's easy to visualize something, but it's harder to project it out.
How do you actually project it out?
Your energy flows and follows your thoughts. It's like molding with clay. I'm watching at the moment, I've not quite reached that stage yet. I know how to do it though.

This description very much supports the idea that all physical forms throughout the universe are the end result of thought-forms and directed energy. Indeed it appears that this applies from the Ultimate Source itself initially manifesting the galaxies and solar systems that populate the universe. Continuing right through to the more detailed creation of all the life forms that inhabit various planets. However, this is not supporting a literal, biblical account of creation. Instead it appears that various blueprints for different animal, vegetable and mineral life forms have been created at various stages along the way. These are constantly evolving in different planetary environments along natural evolutionary lines. Newton provides one example of a subject working to correct a serious imbalance between the dominant animal and plant life forms in the ecosystem of another planet. The process involved using focused thought-forms to give evolution a 'nudge' in the right direction so that the experiment did not have to start afresh. This seems to represent a fine spiritual explanation of the process.

It also appears that to some extent, working with energy is related to healing. In the previous narrative Liam reveals his group are all healers and also energy manipulators. Meanwhile Nadine Castelle attempts to use energy healing in the physical realm in her last life as a doctor. In her review of that life it emerges that in future she will 'need to work with awareness of energy fields and how they affect physical matter'. In line with this, she takes some special time out in the middle of the interlife to do some further energy training. She describes a more subtle process of 'configuration' which is clearly not the same as that of 'creation', and indeed harder to learn:

I'm going to the gardens. I have a special garden I go to. I like to just sit and watch.
What do you do here?
There's lots of things you can do. I like to just try and create form through thoughts.
And what sort of forms do you like to create?

Flowers. They are just thought-forms.

Are there other things you do in this place?

Configuration. Configuring energy frequencies into different forms. You can create different things, different forms of things. Not just matter, but atmospheres. I'm not very good at the moment, I'm just trying to learn it really.

In what way is this different from just creating thought-forms?

Thought-forms are like a telepathic form of turning energy into matter. You can just think of something and pull it down and it becomes matter. With configuration it's purer and you have to understand the subtler types of energy that we create, and under-stand the different types of particle or different types of substance that make the particle into what it is. It's a bit complicated and I will be gaining more understanding of this in the next couple of life forms that I take.

What will you do with this knowledge in your next lives?

Connection. Our group is all about connection, making people feel a certain way, and developing them into a certain type of form. Energetic form that is, so that the human body can open up to the strength of awareness of the spiritual form.

Perhaps the most fascinating aspect of energy work involves operating as a 'light being' who helps to maintain the 'energy matrix' or 'grid' that connects the entire universe. Veronica Perry provides a brief reference to this in her first session when describing one of her life choices:

This option is to continue to channel energies, but in spirit form and above the earth. I'm being shown like a grid where each point is a light being and they're all connected and combining energy.

However Laura Harper provides a far more detailed account when she describes the theme that her group is working on:

Does your group have a particular theme or purpose?
We're developing light radiation.
What does that mean?
What I see in front of me is this matrix all around the earth. This sort of beautiful, beautiful grid, and there are points on it that light up. Actually it's all switched on, they're all lit and joined up. First of all I saw that things on earth like trees and plants, also have this matrix and patterning all joined up. Then from further away, I had a glimpse that all the planets are joined up as well. It's got something to do with 'testing the nodes'.
How does this testing of the nodes work?
We all form a loop, and it's a bit like that film, ET. One of us puts a finger on a node, and the one at the end of the loop has a finger on another node. Just for a moment we become elated or enlightened. It feels like becoming 'charged'. It's a bit like being a light meter.
Hmm, and what happens to the node that you've tapped into?
The node becomes very bright, brilliant. It's a sort of shimmer that goes round, a wave, a pulse. I guess if we get it wrong then it's like some sort of shock. Ah, I see now, we're just conductors from the Source. We act like a kind of charging station. If we didn't do this work, everything on earth would just die, eventually the light would fade. All matter would just become particles, and they wouldn't cohere to make proper form.

Although it is not entirely clear what Laura is getting at here, it does seem that she is at least hinting at the idea of the need for fundamental soul energy. Everything in the universe needs to be maintained and recharged in order for it to remain in coherent physical manifestation.

6

PLANNING THE NEXT LIFE

You are the notes, and we are the flute.
We are the pawns and kings and rooks.
You set out the board: we win or lose.
Jelaluddin Rumi, Sufi mystic, 13th Century.

The crucial idea that we might be actively involved in choosing and planning our own lives is not found in any of the world's religious, spiritual or esoteric traditions. This includes those that adhere to the concept of reincarnation. Surprisingly the first mention of next life planning came as early as the fourth century before Christ. Plato the Greek philosopher referred to a battle wounded soldier's near death experience during which he was offered a choice for the next life. In more modern times the first in-depth account was from an evolved spirit called Seth who spoke via medium Jane Roberts in the nineteen sixties and seventies. However the real thrust behind its emergence has come from interlife research, and all the pioneers report on it without exception. It will be of no surprise that all of the subjects in this research have had some sort of life planning or next life choice.

There are a number of elements to it, and souls may engage in one or more. There may be a degree of forward planning and discussion with spirit guides as early as the past life review or with the soul mates at the group reunion. Some of the previous subject extracts have already covered this. Full planning with soul mates and guides normally happens towards the end of the interlife. At that point there is a preview of the next life, which may come as either a single option or a multiple choice. Finally there is discussion of the next life with the elders to draw on their wider wisdom after a specific choice has been made. However, just as with past-life reviews the specific sequence of events is fluid. In general all that can be said is that the planning elements occur before any review elements.

Most of the subjects were guided to cover their current life preview. To provide a contrast, two of the subjects where allowed to plan for one of their previous lives.

Planning with Other Souls

Emotional problems are involved in both of the following examples of planning meetings. The subject and their soul mates have their respective spirit guides with them. Liam Thompson's planning involves meeting with two soul mates who will be his mother and his best friend. The discussion is about how they can help him with his repetitive suicide problem, and how he can help them too:

I'm going back to my soul group. It's time to discuss things with the two people that I know are coming back with me. We need to discuss the role they will play in helping me achieve what needs to be achieved, and how I can help them, too.

Is anyone else with you?

There's a few spirit guides. Mine and I think they've got their own as well.

Is anybody coming up with ideas about what you're going to do?

Jamie is going to be my very good friend in this life. I'm going to go to school with him. He's eccentric, but he'll keep me balanced. He'll help me see the truth of a situation. I can turn to him quite a lot, because he does speak the truth. Then there's my mum, Karen. She likes to be a mother figure anyway, but she's going to be firm. She won't give in too easily when my life gets too hard and she's going to make me face what I need to face. If I show signs of wanting to get out, to leave and go back home, she's going to know them beforehand and pick them up. So she can help to stop it from happening.

How are you going to help them?

Once I've sorted myself out I'll be like a rock for my mum, because she's got it hard in this life. I will keep Jamie grounded, because he's too much of a free spirit sometimes. Ah, I think I recognize another member of my group. I think it's my sister, and she's with someone else I recognize, Leanne. I need to help her... I have to help my sister as well. I think my guides help by mapping it all out for me.

Liz Kendry's problem over several past lives was undue dependence on her husband and an inability to cope after his death. The same soul mate played the husband role in all of these past lives. In fact he is doing so again in the current life, under the name of Charles. In their planning together they discuss various alternative life situations that will allow her to face the same problem but hopefully handle it better. It also covers how she can help him too:

We talk about being more estranged in our relationship. Another option is we don't find each other, and another is to change roles, but that wouldn't make a difference with losing the other person, the same emotions would still be there. Another is to be in a relationship together where we have to be apart for a lot of the time. That's the one we pick.

What's the reason for picking that and rejecting the others?

In the hope that with this lifetime, if we're spending time apart, we can be together yet still be independent. So we can grow emotionally rather than be dependant on each other.

Is Inka with you?

We're going to see her now. Charles's guide is there too. They think it's a reasonable option.

What does Charles get out of this?

He needs patience. He needs to learn that before the point at which he dies. I have to help him with that and with his children, and everyday life, so he doesn't rush into things. He's going to have opportunities throughout his life where he can 'jump on board' and rush in and it could turn out quite badly, or he could take his time and be very successful. I have to be in there trying to get him to slow down.

The plan is that Charles will die even earlier in this life and leave her to bring up their two children alone. So now we find that they are also involved in the planning process, and that there are special lessons for them too:

I'm wondering why I need the extra challenge of raising two children without their dad at that early stage in their lives. I'm being told that's not my challenge it's theirs.

Do you meet either of those souls and their guides to discuss this with them?

Yes. Isaac doesn't mind, but Claire's really hesitant. She's worried because she'll be older and she'll have a lot more emotional baggage than Isaac. So she's worried about how she will relate to others that do have fathers, or how she will relate to men in general. There's talk of other male role models in their lives. Family members.

At the time of Liz's interlife session, Charles had already passed on as planned. It is therefore important to note that she seems to stick with the original experience in her various meetings with him. It would surely have been tempting for her session to be dominated by her real-time emotions on being reunited with him had she been in full conscious control. Indeed, at no time does she perceive him in real time, and even her joy on her reunion with him that she expressed in chapter 4 was clearly for the personality he had been in their previous past life together. This again suggests a high degree of objectivity in the interlife experience. Neither does this reflect any lack of feelings for Charles in her current life, as her subsequent feedback on the session will later show.

Single Life Previews

Most of the pioneers agree on the general idea of souls having a life preview. This includes information of their future circumstances, such as their parents and geographical location. These are based on prior lives and the lessons to be learnt.

The two subjects who have the most detailed preview of a single life option tend to have a repetitive emotional problem, one not resolved over a number of lives. The first is Liam Thompson's repetitive suicide, and in his report we find that most of his future is withheld in this real-time preview of his life plan:

I'm in like a cinema. [Laughs] It really is a cinema, with seats in rows and a big screen. Except I think I'm in control of what's on the screen and I can see what I want. It's time for me to just have a look at certain things. I'm going to see scenes that will be like pointers for certain events, sort of déjà vu's, so I know I'm on the right track.

What's on these screens?

I see myself finishing university. I've dropped out because it's not right. This has happened already.

What happens next?

I'm working in a bookshop. Actually I work in a bookshop now. Apparently I'm not going to stay there for more than two years.

Are they showing you any events after that?

The tape's running. It's dead.

Is this being blanked out from you?
Yes.
Do you have any other choices of life?
No, I think I've only got this one. I was never given an alternative.
I'm catching up, so I didn't get a chance to pick.
What are your first impressions of this life?
I'm a little bit scared, a little bit apprehensive. I don't want to keep messing up, and I don't want to mess up this one, but I know I've got support.

Of course it would be easy to dismiss this because Liam has exactly the experience we might expect, whereby he only sees things about his current life that have already happened and he knows about. The rest is conveniently blocked. However we will see shortly that those few subjects who plan for a previous past life still obtain the same sort of previews.

It is interesting that Liam makes the unusual suggestion that the events he sees in this preview will act as subconscious 'triggers' for him to know he is on the right track when incarnate. It makes sense that if we see ourselves doing certain jobs or other activities in our life preview, we should obtain a feeling of déjà vus once we are actually engaged in them in the physical realm.

Jack Hammond, who is working on not being a loner, is in something of a hurry to come back to incarnation after only a brief reunion with his soul group. This is more common following a life when a core issue was either incompletely learnt or missed entirely. It is almost as if the soul wants to quickly apply the insight from the previous failure and rectify the problem. Jack's description of the life preview process is detailed and engaging:

I've got to go back and do it again.
Ok, so where do you go?

Somewhere different. I know I'm preparing to reincarnate. I don't know whether I actually like it that much.

Just describe the place that you're in at the moment.

The first word that comes to mind is like a cockpit. No, not a cockpit, an operations room. I really struggle to describe some of these places.

Is this in energy form like the other places?

Yes. It's like there's just a vague hint of an instrument panel, although it's like no instrument panel I know. It's more like these things are here to convey something, rather than to do something. This is where they map it all out for the next life.

What's actually happening in this room?

There's at least two other people here. They're working the instruments, or whatever they are, and I'm being shown where I'm going. It's interesting, but I don't have to go, I don't have to do this.

What are they actually showing you?

One or two of the things I'm not going to like. I'm going to have exactly the same mum and dad.

Is this being shown you or are you actually experiencing the life?

It's a mixture of both. To describe it in the language I have, it's like I'm looking at the screen, but its really not that simple.

What's your first impression of the life?

My mother is part Maori, which means I'm going to be as well. Somehow I'll be different, although I don't know why. Oh! I get it, I get it. I'm going to be a poor little Maori boy. My brother and sister aren't. With me the Maori genes will come through and I'm going to be dark-skinned. My mother is not going to be too pleased with a child that turns the gene, so I think I'll be a source of disappointment.

How is this going to help you with your life's purpose?

It looks like I'm going to be cast out. I'm going to have every excuse in the world to be a loner, and to be by myself. That's where I've got to start from, but I've got to learn to give. I'm going to be given some attributes. I'm going to have a great sporting ability, which means I'll meet a lot of people, so it's going to be a chance to give of myself. There's something else, something else. It's a sensitivity. It's going to be a love of human nature.

Are these attributes coming from your past lives or from some other source?

They're things I've had before but I've repressed them. They've always been there. So I can either choose to use them, or do what I've always done before and turn in on myself. The challenge is going to be tough, very tough.

Are you given any choices, or is only one life being shown?

I have the choice not to go at all, but there's a determined streak in me. I don't really like what I've got to do, but I don't want to stay where I am. The impression I'm getting is that it's not an order. Don't get the wrong idea, but it's like 'Here's a good scenario for you, think about it carefully. You know that this is the best. You're being well set up with everything you need, but you are going to be challenged.' I've got a hell of a lot of apprehension, but it's different from human apprehension.

What does Garth think about this life?

He's just smiling at me. It's like, 'you'll survive, you'll be fine'.

Here Jack provides an excellent confirmation of a point made by several of the pioneers. If a soul is given only one life option that is not attractive to them they may initially reject the idea. It could be assumed that souls can be forced into a life that they do not want. Further probing always confirms that this is not the case and they can turn it down. What actually happens is that even less experienced souls usually take a little time to appreciate that this is what they need, if they are to make any proper progress and to break free from repetitive patterns of behavior.

Although these are the most detailed single life previews experienced by the subjects they are not the only ones. For example, when Nicola Barnard meets her elders she is only given one choice. More significantly, we saw in the previous chapter how Lene Haugland engages in a variety of more intellectual pursuits in the light realms. This suggests that she is a reasonably experienced soul and does not appear to have any sort of repetitive emotional problem. Nevertheless, she too is only offered one choice: 'I know what life I'm going to live... There are no options... It's just so important that I go into that family.' It therefore seems that it would be wrong to associate a lack of life choices with a low level of soul experience.

Multiple Choice Previews

Only Newton discusses in detail the idea of souls having a choice of more than one potential life. The subjects fully confirm his findings, and approximately three-quarters of those who experienced a preview reported they had a multiple life choice.

There are a number of excellent examples of these previews. Nadine Castelle has a brief discussion with her spirit guide about life choices at a very early stage, during her initial review after her life as a doctor:

My spirit guide says I have choices. To go back into the medical profession to increase awareness, or to go into another profession that will increase awareness. I chose the latter, the medical one felt too heavy, and I would have had to become male again and I didn't want to.

For most subjects the preview comes towards the end of their interlife. Perhaps coincidently, nearly all of those that are quoted had three lives to choose from. In the first of these, Katja Eisler, chooses the life that has the most possibilities. We will recall she had the past life as the Mexican peasant with more regard for his donkey than people. She is with Merlo her guide, although he does not seem to be too involved in the process:

I can feel an eagerness to come back into the physical life again.

So what do you do?

I'm leaving my group, saying goodbye. There's no need to hug them, we feel so connected they know I care. There is a big white building, big walls, flat top, white, big doors, and inside there are stages.

Do you know what this building is?

It's to see the bodies, or scenes. I have a glimpse into a life.

How are they presented to you?

I move round the stages. They are made of wood, not very big, like in a small theatre.

How do they work?

I'm not sure if I'm supposed to stay at the front or go round the back to see what's there. I can see Merlo, he's a little bit behind me, and when I look at him he's telling me 'you can decide this alone, you will know'.

So what do you do?

I see a girl in Japan. It's more like a film than a theatre. She's very tiny and fragile.

Is her life presented to you?

Her father is very strict and her mum dies early.

Why do you reject this option?

Maybe it's too difficult because she's so fragile. I see a second wife of the father and she's very strict as well.

What's the next option?

My life. My body. It will be unwanted by its mother as a child, but having a deep connection to the father. Having to learn a lot of empathy with the mother. A lot about betrayal. Betrayal of the father and of others. To betray and to be betrayed.

What attracts you to this life?

I can sense a very strong will connected with this body, and a flexible mind. I wouldn't call this life easy, but there are more possibilities.

Are you shown any other possibilities?

Yes, a boy, his body looks very clumsy. I'm shown a very shy personality, very insecure, of this boy and of this man. It's like it would maybe be in England or Ireland. The family are living a very simple life, very underprivileged, not much capacity to build on.

So why do you reject it?

The boy has a lot of learning difficulties. I thought I could influence more with the one before.

Are you shown any more options?

That's it.

And do you discuss this with Merlo?

He knows, he agrees.

We can see that Katja is considering lives on different continents, as does Marta Petersen who had the altruistic life as the Jewish girl in the Second World War:

I'm at the place of body selection. I have a table in front of me, it bends inwards towards me so I am almost surrounded.

Are you by yourself?

Yes, but I think my guide is going to join me later.

How many bodies can you choose from?

Three.

So just go through the two options that you didn't take.

The first one is a boy from Oslo, in Norway.

Is it a strong or weak body?

Weak. He has a tendency to get overweight but a lot of potential musically.

Why do you reject it?

Because physically it doesn't look like what I have in mind. I would miss out on important lessons if I looked like this.

What are these lessons that you would miss out on?

I would isolate myself a bit, I wouldn't get a lot of sexual experiences, and this is something that I appreciate very much when I have a chance to practice it.

In what way are sexual experiences important for you?

I have to get better at controlling my emotions, and this is one way for me to get stronger in myself. This boy would not have many sexual partners because he is not very attractive.

Ok, go to the next body and describe that?

This is a girl, in China or Japan, but I rule this out almost immediately because their way of living doesn't suit me. They are somewhat narrow-minded, at least where this body would grow up. My spiritual growth would not be very significant here, because then I would be too involved with making a career out of my music. It's a big puzzle because I have a lot of things I want to learn in this one life.

Now turn to the body you choose, and tell me your feelings about it?

It's challenging, because I would stand out a lot. I am tall. I would not have the ability to blend in very well and from a very early age I would stand out.

Is this a strong body?

It's medium. It's not a body where I'm going to do a lot of sport and suchlike, but it's strong enough.

Do you have a choice of emotions to go with this body?

Well, it's a very stubborn body, I will not be able to hide my emotions, and I can see how people are going to react around me.

Do you discuss this choice with your spirit guide?

Yes. He says there are a couple of things I need to think through. There will be some significant points in my life where I have a choice to give up or to continue. If I can get through them it will be ok, but there's a risk that I might not make it.

What are these significant points?

There's going to be a difficult time in my teens, and he's thinking of sending someone to help me. I will have low self-esteem at this time. I have to experience some things very early because otherwise I won't be able to make the most of this life.

By contrast, Laura Harper seems to concentrate more on the emotional make-up of what are in her four options. We will recall she had the past life of the old man whose town was invaded and was learning not to take life so seriously:

I feel like I'm in a room in a sort of space ship or something. It's round and it's dark. There are consoles, and there are four sort of black slabs of marble or something. They're used for the bodies I could inhabit.

Just go through the bodies one by one and tell me what your impression of them is?

Ok, the first one is a woman. Quite small and slight, very finely boned. Too fragile.

How would that body help you for your purpose in this life?

Um, that body actually has very delicate, receptive, sensitivity. That person is very finely tuned and looks too fragile for words, but actually has a very fine receptivity.

What does that mean for the sort of life you would have?

It would not be an easy life. She would be very finely tuned to healing work. She would be marvelous.

Why did you reject this body?

She's too fragile. She's not robust.

Would it be a very difficult life with that body?

Her fine tuning means she's also very sensitive to being too easily bruised and the word mutilated comes in.

Go to the second one.

The second one is almost exactly the opposite. It's a man, tall and strong and really very strikingly beautiful with long hair, looks a bit Nordic. A bit like a Viking.

Why did you reject this one?

It would be very hard to be sensitive enough to fulfill my contract. It would be very tempting to squander my life on superficial things.

Go onto the third choice then.

It's a woman. Dark haired. She's quite a fiery one. I can see she also knows hatred. She's quite fun. Now I have to think why I would not choose her. The word that comes to mind is 'willful'.

Would it be an easy or a hard life if you were in this body?

It would be quite easy. It would actually be quite fun.

Would it give you the spiritual development you're looking for?

No. No, there's a lot of resistance in that body to softening.

Go onto the fourth body. What is it that appealed to you about that body?

I'm seeing this body. Uh, she's also a bit of a wild one, she's not quite as finely tuned as the first, but she has a fine sensitivity about her. I can see that she has something of that other willfulness, she feels challenging.

Just remind me what your soul purpose is for this life?

My soul purpose is to bring love.

How will she help with this?

She has a robust nature, but she has anxiety that feels like it's very finely balanced. Like there is a sense of riding a very high-spirited horse that needs a careful management.

Are you by yourself when you look at these bodies, or is your spirit guide or teacher with you?

She is, yes. I hadn't noticed, but she is, she's here to my right.

Do you have any discussion about the level of intelligence that goes with this body?

[Laughs] She warns me that her condition in life will make her like a charged battery that her life path will not be an easy one, with that amount of emotion.

It has already been mentioned that a potential criticism of interlife planning is that the subject consciously knows about one of the options, which is their current life. However, we now move to two interlife regressions in which the subjects plan for a previous life in their sequence of past lives. In these interlives, none of the options could have been known about in advance.

The first of these follows Veronica Perry's past life in which she dies in bed at the age of 86 after the relatively unchallenging life. She is offered interesting and very different type of lives. One option is to remain in the spirit realms and continue learning to work with energy, and the other two options are physical lives. Of particular importance is her minimal prior knowledge:

I've got three choices.

Tell me about the choices?

I have two options for physical form or I can stay in energy form.

Ok, go through each option.

The first physical option is to incarnate as an orphan, a little girl. It's like I'm having a picture of this little girl put inside my mind.

What aspect would you learn about in this particular body?

This would be a very difficult life. [sighs] I can't see any learning for me in this life, this is more about teaching.

How would it be teaching?

It's about trying to bring some focus onto the hardship and the horrors that can happen with children. [sighs]

What are your overall thoughts and impressions about that sort of life?

I don't think anybody really wants that sort of life.

Ok, let's move onto the second option.

Hmm. This second life is one where I can continue my learning on patience. I'm not being given too much information about that life because it's a life where I need to learn.

What sort of person would you be?

I'd be male, from a quite wealthy family, but there is patience and tolerance to be learnt.

And what's your impression about that life?

I feel attracted to it because of the learnings. These are feelings that I still need to experience. I reject it because there will be other opportunities to have those learnings.

Ok, now go onto the third option.

This is to continue to channel energies but in spirit form and above the earth. I'm being shown, like a grid. A grid where each point on the grid is a light being and they're all connected and combining energy, and I can go and join them.

What are your thoughts about that option?

I think that would be nice, but I reject it. Although I know it will be hard, I feel I have to take the first option. I've just had a gift of a life. A peaceful joyous life, and I feel that I can have a harder option this time.

It's interesting that Veronica picked the life plan of the orphan despite in her words, 'I don't think anybody really wants that sort of life'. The implication of a life for the benefits of others, called an altruistic life, will be examined later. Meanwhile, after David Stephen's short life as the Arab robbed and left to die in the desert, we find him planning for a previous life in the Victorian era. There are unusual aspects of this wonderfully specific report. He starts with as many as a dozen options that are quickly reduced to three. Also he finds himself previewing these lives not only with his guide Gendar, but also in conjunction with several of his closest soul mates. This gives a clear element of group planning as well. Understandably, given the situation he refers to them by their spiritual rather than their earthly names:

All three of us are there. That's unusual, they are the ones I will be working with. There are lots of screens around and they are very fluid and I know I can step in at any point. It's interesting, just by touching the screen you get a flavor of that person's life. You can kind of jump into it.

Are these future lives?

Yes. There are quite a few lives, maybe a dozen. We quickly remove several of them and now there are three. I'm with Marcus and Zendos. My guide Gendar is there as well, and he is moving towards a particular life. Oh, it's a life in Victorian England as an upper class woman. I know that's the one I'll choose. It's the contradictions in it. It's the privilege and yet the pain of losing a child in childbirth and almost dying, and then not being able to have children afterwards.

In what way would that be of help to you?

It's not just me, it's for Marcus as well.

In what way would it help him?

It's about dealing with loss, about dealing with grief, about whether our relationship can survive an experience like that. What we learn about our own ability to forgive, to let go.

Will any other soul group members be involved with that aspect of your life?

Marcus usually takes a stern role in my lives. We have this

agreement to have similar roles. Marcus will be my husband. I realize another aspect to do with Marcus is to work with his sexual needs, because I'm not able or willing to have sex after the child dies. So a big challenge for him will be how he copes with that, from being in a young loving relationship to having to deal with this trauma.

He then moves on to discuss the role that Zantos, another soul mate will play. Not only does he agree to have an altruistic life in which he is the baby that is stillborn, but it seems that he may then incarnate again swiftly as an orphan who David will look after:

And the child, do you know who that will be?
Yes it will be Zantos, he will come along for this one.
What will your other soul group members be gaining by their experiences?
For Zantos it's more about what he can give rather than gain from that life. He has his own issues to work through, particularly around anger, but he will be working as a healer and needs to bring it into body form. I support an orphanage in my later years, and I support him in that life. For Marcus it's about rejection and intimacy. It's like we need this to really push ourselves to see if we can survive something rather shocking for us, and still do what we need to do.
Do you discuss this with your spirit guide?
Yes, very much so, he is an integral part of our discussions.
Are there any aspects that you adjust?
No. It seems right. It has all the likely outcomes, in particular the death of the child.

Planning with the Elders
As discussed previously these are evolved spirits who have no need to

reincarnate, and normally offer a deeper level of knowledge and insight than spirit guides. They are encountered in groups often referred to as a 'council,' and usually assist in planning for the next life and the final review before incarnation. Some subjects appear comfortable to perceive them in their normal energy form, while others prefer to perceive them adopting a semi-human appearance. In this case the gender can be either male or female. Often they are seen wearing ornaments that have a symbolic meaning for the soul before them.

The subjects who met with their elders twice in one session found the composition of the council was the same. However, it appears that it can change from one interlife to the next. Meanwhile Newton stresses that the composition of the council is different for each member of any given soul group. Although there is no information from this research to confirm this, it is consistent with how elders operate.

Despite her minimal prior knowledge, Nicola Barnard the earthquake victim provides a fine report of her planning meeting. Although by the end she does change her initial expectation that she is going to have to make choices:

> Choices have to be made in this place. Decisions about how it's going to be this time. There's probably only three, four or five of these light beings, and they are supporting the choices to be made… They are very wise… I feel a bit in awe. There's a sense that they know so much. And they are very, very kind, hugely compassionate… There's a sense of finding out what still needs to be done and to be experienced. It's all about the experience, and experiencing… They know all about your past lives, that's one of the things that is so awesome about them… It's kind of like a council... I don't feel like there are choices actually, I merely feel that I am going to be a girl… They are telling me I need to stay

safe. When I'm little I won't think that I'm safe, but I will be. I think that's what they want me to know.

Liz Kendry is somewhat unique in that she is one of the few subjects to experience both a review and a planning meeting with her elders separately. Although she confirms that on both occasions the council's composition is the same, and she primarily communicates with the same lead figure. This meeting does not cover her repetitive problems with her soul partner, Charles, but instead concentrates on other aspects of her emotional learning for the life to come:

I outline my next life, and the purpose and the goals that I intend to meet, and the purpose of the soul group, and I talk to him about the selection of the body... There will be some other life challenges that they'll be able to give me, and my spirit guide will be able to help me overcome some of those... It's to do with me having to say what I think rather than shielding people... So rather than sparing people's feelings, I have to consider my own feelings first...There will be occasions such as relationships I'll have along the way that will be a test, they won't be good, and rather than sticking with them and taking the emotional hurt that comes with them, I have to speak up... There's going to be a time when I'm young and some men are going to try and get me in their car and I have to be strong and say no. There's other examples, like friend-ships and friends that may be a little abusive in their words to me, or insensitive in the way they talk to me. It may happen only occasionally, and most of the time those friendships will be pretty sound. I must not override the hurt that is there. Something has to be said. There'll be lots of tests along the way until I finally get it... These are new learnings for me.

Liam Thompson is also somewhat unique in that he meets his elders to plan his next life before his planning meeting with his soul group and his life preview. This meeting turns out to be more of a general discussion on his progress and problems. We now find that as well as being in training as a healer, he is also nearly a guide despite his problems with suicide. The issue of his repetitive problems causing his progress to fall behind his group is discussed. Even though he expresses some preliminary concern about the meeting, as usual we find that the elders adopt a balanced and loving approach. He refers to the elders as higher people:

Where do you go next?
It's like a cathedral. A leaning cathedral, with glass, twinkling. Everything twinkles and glimmers.
Is someone with you?
I think I'm by myself at this point. I'm going to discuss something important.
Who is it you're going to discuss this important thing with?
It's like a council of higher people. They're my council. I can see five of them.
And is your spirit guide with you?
Behind me. He just stays out of the way. He's an observer, so we can discuss this in more detail later on. He's doing this for me, because he knows I need to hear it. I'm going to get pushed now.
Are these council members in energy form or human form?
In human form.
Do you sense one of them is more prominent than the others?
Yes. He's wearing a really dark purple robe. He's got a bald head, white around the sides. He's quite small and podgy. His nose is quite big, flat on his face, the eyes are very piercing. I don't get the impression of a color, just that they hold a lot of wisdom.
Tell me what happens between you?
He's encouraging my uniqueness, and telling me about my ability.

He's telling me about where my soul group members are in their development. He says they're all progressing very nicely, but unfortunately I'm keeping them back. So, he's telling me that I need to pick my next life, and I need to pick it soon. Otherwise I'm not going to catch up. Either that, or he's giving me the option of moving behind. We're not forced to do anything.

What would that involve?

Going to another group. A far less developed one. I'm practically at guide level myself, so I don't want to go and fall behind.

What else do they discuss with you?

They tell me that two of the members of my soul group, the two people I've already recognized, have agreed to come back. There's a couple more as well, but I haven't met them yet.

Do they tell you what the purpose of this life is going to be?

I need to help a lot of other people as well, and to stop indulging myself. I'm a caring soul though, very caring. We're all caring in my group. Also I need to find my own happiness within myself, before I can find it with anybody else. I always look for somebody else to fill the void when it needs to be filled by myself first.

These last wise words are something we can all learn from. Liam also emphasizes the point made by Jack Hammond earlier in this chapter that we are not forced to reincarnate at all. He also reports separately that 'our guides know when it's time, and we become restless, and they don't make us return, but they encourage it by showing the benefits'.

As usual Veronica Perry with minimal prior knowledge provides a detailed account of meeting her elders prior to her past incarnation as an orphan. It seems to be relatively informal, and designed to provide maximum encouragement and support for what will be a very difficult life:

We've agreed on the life I'm going to have next, and my spirit guide and I are going to go and talk to the council of elders about it.

Just describe the appearance of the place.

This is another dome but much bigger. It's all made from light but it looks like marble. I feel twelve energies.

What position are they relative to you?

They're higher up in front of me. I always feel so small. They're stood on, um, it's like a big step going half way around the dome... My spirit guide and I are standing together.

What is it you can see?

Although they're in human form they're much longer, taller and radiating some light. There are some very tall-backed chairs and there is a very long table. They're not sitting there today.

Do you sense one of these elders is more prominent than the others?

Yes, there's one further forward.

Have a close look at the face and describe the face to me?

It's a very kind face and the features aren't prominent. It's sort of half in light form and half in human form.

Just be aware of any ornament or anything that's being shown you?

There's a staff. It looks like a very soft wood but it has a very bright, very big crystal at the top of it.

What's the significance to you of this staff with the crystal on top?

It's a sign of a hierarchy, but the softness of it shows that it's also friendship and a compassionate, um, leadership.

Does this one communicate to you?

This elder has taken a vaguely female form and she tells me that she's pleased about my choice.

How did this elder know about your choice?

They tend to know anyway. We're all linked.

Do they say anything else to you?
It's quite informal telling me that they're generally pleased with the work that's being done, and they're glad that I enjoyed the last life. They know it was a very difficult choice to make for the next life but there are lots of souls being asked to make these difficult choices.

Discussed in the last section was David Stephens's review of his choices before having his next past life as a woman in Victorian England. When asked if he needs to meet the 'spirits of light who plan new lives' before he reincarnates, he says 'no, we have discussed it enough already'. Just to illustrate the flexibility of the interlife experience he is told to 'go to another point between lives when you meet the spirits of light that do the final checks', and he switches to a different interlife altogether. This time he finds himself meeting 'wise ones' that are not his normal elders, before a past life some time ago in Greece. In complete contrast to Veronica, we find that at this point he has had a succession of hard lives because he has been anxious to gain experience as fast as possible. So this time he is being offered an easy one as a sort of 'holiday' even though he appears to protest that he does not deserve it:

This is quite a long time ago, this is before my life in Greece, and it is going to be quite a wonderful life in many ways. Not without its challenges, but with great love and spiritual understanding in it... I feel as if I don't deserve it. I have been following a sequence of hard lives because I want to really deepen my understanding of what I am quickly. I feel the way to do it is to have tough, challenging lives but this one was chosen for me, almost like a holiday. I'm saying that I don't deserve it, but they are saying 'you have earned it, and you will deepen your understanding of yourself'.

Recaps, Reminders and Triggers

One of the ideas put forward by Newton's clients is that souls get together for a final recap session in which certain triggers will be agreed that will help them to recognize each other back on the earth realms. This is a specific instance of the more general idea of making plans with our soul group that we have already discussed, and a number of our subjects corroborate it. For example, Nadine Castelle briefly reports on the following exchange during her initial reunion with her soul group:

> They're teasing me that when we come back into the next life we will all recognize each other but in different ways.

The specific idea of a recap is hinted at more strongly by Liz Kendry, who reports briefly on further discussions with her soul group that occur before she meets with her elders:

> We just get together to talk about who is who and the inter-relationships and the timing.

By contrast, Marta Petersen reports on discussions with another soul who is not from her group but will be her husband in the life to come. In this case he specifically projects the body he will have when she meets him, presumably as a pretty effective aid for her to recognize him:

> I'm meeting another soul. He's going to be my future husband, and he shows himself in the body in which I will meet him.
> *Describe him for me?*
> He's tall like myself. It's the man I met when I was eighteen. He's from another group. We have great understanding of each other, we have worked together before. He tells me that I don't have to be

afraid that I'm going to miss him, because he's going to hang on when he meets me. He will only be my husband for a short time, because he has another purpose for his life.

How will he help you?

He will comfort me when I feel most alone, and he will give up a lot of things for me, but he will also challenge me.

In real time Marta realized who the person is and had met him, but they are not yet partners, let alone married. This raises the interesting question of whether this experience will have influenced her future life choices. However, given the blocking about future information that has been previously encountered it can be certain that she would not have been allowed to recall this part of the experience unless it would be useful to her in some way.

Liam Thompson has the most complete planning recall of all the subjects. He has a planning meeting with his elders, then his soul group and then his life preview. Finally he has this recap discussion with other souls both within and outside his group. What follows is an excellent detailed description of the process:

I'm just running over more important events in my life with my soul group so I know that when I meet them they are people from my group. My guide is also showing me other people who will be in my life, from other groups. I can assist them.

Tell me who you're being shown?

My Nan, and my granddad, and someone who will be a very big learning curve in my life. Heather will be my first proper relationship. It's finished now anyway. It finished a while ago. She helps me to go to university because I need to be given the strength and confidence of living away from my family. She encourages me to do my A-levels and helps me to get to university. We're going to be very close.

Is there anything else that you're permitted to know?

Hmm. It's going to be very hard when we part. At the same time, I'm assisting her as well. It's a two-way process. I help her to grow up. She's very naïve and in the same sort of position I am. She gives up too easily. That's why we were brought together. She's been in my life before. Not my most recent one, a few before then. I was her father, trying to help her to grow up then as well. She'll always be the child.

Have you finished with this meeting?

There's lots of people around, and I'm just going over everyone who'll have a big impact in my life. So many people that I open myself up, and they do the same to me. It's like telepathy, but it's more than that. I'm expressing everything, and they're expressing everything. Lessons, things I need to learn, things I need to work on. It's sort of like a brief overview of what's to come. There are a lot of people who're going to help.

Clearly Liam is swapping back and forward between original and real time in this excerpt, just as he was during his life preview. His description seems far more insightful than a mere recounting of things he already knows. For example, he recognizes that he has been with Heather in a previous life, although not his most recent one.

Lisbet Halvorsen describes being allowed the privileged access of a library of life books. These allow her access to the future life options of other souls. The reason for this is that she is learning how to assist in the planning of their lives:

I can open the middle door and it's the biggest. It's curved, and inside there are lots of scrolls. It looks like a big library, with scrolls for every soul.

What do the scrolls look like?

They are rolled up, but when you open them you see everything like a movie, and you get all the information you need on every soul. All the lives it's had, where it's at now, how it's progressing.

What are you coming in here to do?

It's like I'm allowed to go in and look at the scrolls. I'm researching and learning about how they work.

Have you been here before?

I've been here a few times and it's a big honor. They trust me when I do this and I'm eager and excited. I'm going to plan lives, look at how things work together and match up.

How will this knowledge help?

To see where people and things are heading, and what souls need to learn according to what they have been doing. So I read the file and see what they are missing. What would be good to do next, and who wants to work with whom.

How do you do this?

It's like people are arranged into different groups, so you can tell who can go together. They are in soul groups, but what is more difficult is to work with bigger groups and how a big group can work together. To see if they have a plan, and how that fits with the bigger plan.

Are there lots of possibilities?

Yes. It's about seeing a wholeness and seeing what's best so everyone can learn what they need to. I think about it, then I see the solution and I see if it is good or bad. Then I may not pick that one, then I pick another one, and think about it, and think 'yeah, that'll be good'. It's a bit difficult, so maybe I'm just in the learning process of doing this.

This is an excellent and detailed account, and all that can be added by way of commentary is that to the human mind her description of this planning being 'a bit difficult' is something of an understatement.

Before leaving this chapter it is worth stressing that interlife regression is more than a spiritual journey. Touching the energies and wisdom of the elders has a deep and lasting effect on people. Having meaning and purpose to life is a powerful psychological resource.

7

KARMIC DYNAMICS

This earth is neither the beginning
nor the end of your existence.
It is simply a step, a schoolroom.
Emmanuel, channeled through medium Pat Rodegast.

At this point it is useful to bring together aspects of karma from some of the previous chapters and put them into context. Of particular importance is the reason why we reincarnate, and what it means for us in our everyday lives.

Learning, Experience and Growth

The traditional ideas of karma as a process of 'action and reaction', 'paying off debts' or 'reaping what you sow' are simply a surface level view. It's understandable to come to the conclusion that if someone puts out violence in their current life they inevitably get violence directed back. They attract back to themselves what they put out into the world. Also it may appear that a soul exhibiting a pattern of being a victim over many lives is paying off the debts of some misdemeanor in a past life. However interlife allows us to see these situations in a different, and more flexible perspective.

We have already seen that our subjects repeatedly refer to ideas of learning, experience and growth, and this is perhaps best illustrated by Nicola Barnard's comment that:

It's all about the experience, and experiencing.

Liam Thompson's repetitive suicide problem has been reviewed at some length. He himself indicates that this is still part of his learning and growth, even if it is a lesson he is struggling with. It is also hard to see how there could be any element of reaction or debt repayment in his succession of suicide lives. Neither did his spirit guide talk about it in these terms. He merely faces similar situations to see if he will learn not to take the easy way out:

> He's asking me why I always take the easy way out. I have a problem with facing problems... I don't get angry, but he needs to understand that I need an easier life now. I'm sick of doing these really hard ones... He tells me I need to stop thinking about things so much. I need to just learn to live.

A number of the subjects faced similar repetitive problems. For example at the end of her elder review Liz Kendry without prompting, revealed that her problem was giving up after the death of her husband:

> It's happened before... Three times... It's always my husband dying, and then I feel there's no life to live afterwards.... They're going to give me more help next time... They will let it be known to me, through other people or my own consciousness that we don't die when our bodies die, so I won't feel that loss as I have in previous lives.

She also discussed how she and her close soul mate made plans to help her to break this pattern in her current life. In fact this same soul has played the role of her husband in each of the past lives in which she has faced this problem. The final example is Jack Hammond, whose problem also concerns the way he treats other people. In the middle of his elder review he too reveals that this is a lesson he has been working on over the course of several lives:

> I'm sensing that, for want of a better word, there's a disapproval, because I did have opportunities and I did what I've done before in other lives. Disapproval is probably too strong a word though.

There is no evidence in this research that less experienced souls are treated differently from more experienced ones, although some may not listen to the advice offered. All the subjects reported they got help from their spirit guide and elders for their learning and spiritual growth.

The Role of Freewill

This is an appropriate time to review freewill in the context of learning. We have seen that key events in the life plan can be discussed and agreed between soul group members, including the different roles they will take. This includes pre-agreed triggers that at a subconscious level in our human existence compel us to be drawn to certain people and activities. Finally the life plan is reviewed with elders and extra wisdom added, including taking into account the life plans of other souls. When we do incarnate according to Marta Petersen 'spirit guides can give people ideas and encourage them to stay on the life plan at any time'. Understandably it might appear that our lives are completely fixed and predetermined.

However, at a soul level no life plan is forced on a soul. As Liam Thompson reported, 'we're not forced to do anything'. A soul can remain in the spirit realms rather than incarnate and continue the learning from there. However, as Jack Hammond commented about the reluctance to accept a life plan, 'we become restless and our spirit guide encourages it by showing the benefits'. We will recall David Stephens who was even reluctant in accepting the life plan which was 'like a holiday' after a series of 'hard lives'. The elders explained that it would help 'deepen his understand of himself'. Of the other subjects in the last chapter, many had multiple life options with different grades of difficulty. This all confirms the amount of freewill our souls have in accepting any life plan.

Of course in human existence our conscious mind likes to think we have freewill over everything. Over many things it does, but interlife evidence shows that the key events in our life plan have a major probability of happening. As Liz Kendry reported, 'There will be occasions such as relationships I'll have along the way that will be a test and they won't be good. Rather than sticking with them and taking the emotional hurt that comes with them, I have to speak up'. We have freewill to respond to our life plan, to either prolong suffering or complete our learning. As Liz continued, 'There'll be lots of tests along the way until I finally get it.'

Emotional Lessons and Specialist Skills

There appear to be two broad themes of learning that a soul can work on, both as an individual and in groups. The first is developing a specialist skill such as becoming a healer, teacher or spirit guide. The second is learning emotional skills that involve experiencing both sides of different emotions. There are a number that have to be learnt, such as to take responsibility, to be loved, to have power and to be a victim. All the emotions must be covered. So for example in one life a soul may have to use the emotion of anger and be in touch with it. Then in another have anger directed on them by another. Experiencing the emotions from those different perspectives continues until the lesson is learnt.

None of the pioneers seem to make any proper distinction between these two types of soul theme. It could be assumed that less experienced souls work on emotional lessons, while the mature ones work on more specialist skills. A close inspection of the evidence suggests this would be wrong, because at least some more experienced souls appear to be addressing both themes simultaneously.

Veronica Perry's three life choices is an example of this. Her first option is staying in spirit form working in the energy matrix surrounding the earth:

> This is to continue to channel energies but in spirit form and above the earth. I'm being shown, like a grid. A grid where each point on the grid is a light being and they're all connected and combining energy, and I can go and join them.

This would seem to indicate a specialist skill rather than an emotional lesson. However another option she had was to carry on working on the emotional lesson of patience that clearly shows that the two themes overlap:

> This second one is where I can continue my learnings on patience. I'm not being given too much information about that life because it's a life where I need to learn.

Marta Petersen, following her death as a Jew in WW2, seems to represent a similar mixture. When she is considering her current life choices she still has many lessons she wants to work on, including 'being better at emotional control'. Yet a little later we find her in a classroom with 8 students and she appears to be training to be a teacher:

> I like to work by talking about an experience I have had in one of my lives, and discussing it with the students. Then they give their view of what they would have done in that situation, and we talk about choices and so on.

Moving to Liam Thompson who is still working on his repetitive suicide problem. He is in training to be a healer as his specialist skill together with his group, and is also nearly at guide level:

> They're creating with their energy. They're all healers. I am as well.

The subject that sheds the most light on the blending of emotional and specialist skills is Wendy Simpson, who in the past life was an old man in the desert. One of the personal lessons she has been repeatedly working on over several lives is her treatment of others. After her elder review, and despite her minimal prior knowledge of the interlife, she describes rejoining her soul group. Here she talks about the specialist skills they are working on together:

> Apart from the lessons that we are experiencing, this group has other things to do. It's about communication. We are working with light energies, and using sound and vibration. In our physical lives we all try to help other people with herbs, oils, healing, and even just by walking from place to place and communicating with them.

It is clear that Wendy's whole group is working on emotional lessons and specialist skills at the same time.

Altruistic Lives
Both Newton and Cannon use the term 'filler lives' when a client talks about a life not necessary for their own learning. These are normally of fairly short duration and their primary aim is to assist another soul's karmic development rather than one's own. A slightly more accurate description is to call them an altruistic life.

A good example of this comes from Marta Petersen, who regresses to a past life as a young Jewish girl in Warsaw in WW2. When German soldiers came to take her parents away, her father insists that she should stay and hide. She does this, but after a few days she is discovered and ends up on the same train as her parents. She is taken to the gas chambers and dies in her mother's arms. In her review with her spirit guide we intriguingly find that her soul perspective on this apparently tragic life was not too difficult at all:

We don't have a lot to talk about because this life was very short, and I was there because of another person. So I did what I was supposed to do.

What was that?

I was going to assist Tina [her mother in that life].

And how did you assist her?

She has a problem with harmonizing her own energy and gets affected by others. So I was there to remind her to focus her energy, and to be with her at the time of our death. When she looked at me and looked into my eyes and felt my energy she was reminded of that energy that she should try to have.

Was this something you had worked out beforehand?

Yes, and the harmonies from the piano also helped her. We work a lot with musical harmonies.

What other sort of things are you reviewing?

If I assisted her enough and if I could have done a better job. I feel very satisfied and I think he [spirit guide] is too. Um. He says that I could have ignored my father's wish and not hid, and gone to the concentration camp earlier with my parents. He asks me why I chose to stay behind.

What do you say?

I wanted to give her a chance on her own, and it felt like the right thing to do was to leave her. Of course I wasn't aware of this when I was incarnated but something told me to hide and not go with her.

What does your guide say about this?

He says it was an interesting choice.

Marta's description of being in that life 'because of another person' is of vital importance in understanding that this is an altruistic life rather than one for her own karmic emotional learning.

8

RETURNING TO INCARNATION

Our birth is but a sleep and a forgetting.
The soul that rises with us, our life star,
has had elsewhere its setting
and cometh from afar.
William Wordsworth.

Selecting Energies, Emotions and Strengths

Newton is the only pioneer who properly discusses the idea that we leave a portion of our soul energy behind in the light realms when we reincarnate. One point that he emphasizes is that the soul does not completely split because each part retains the entire experience of the whole. In some ways it resembles a hologram. He further proposes that more experienced souls need to bring less with them into the physical realm because their energy is generally more 'concentrated' or 'potent'. So he suggests that, whereas the average soul might bring down somewhere between fifty and seventy percent, a more experienced soul may bring down as little as twenty-five percent. Finally, he makes the point that once this level of energy has been agreed in the light realms it cannot be 'topped up' once the soul is incarnate.

Generally speaking the subjects appear to corroborate Newton's research. The amount of energy brought into incarnation is a compromise. If too much is brought down the soul perspective would simply overwhelm the human nervous system, and it may result in the person not fully engaging in the human experience. On the other hand, if too little is brought down for a difficult life the risk is a failure of the life plan. However, we will find out that sometimes souls are able to draw upon some of the energy reserves of their own higher self, soul group or spirit guides in a crisis.

The less experienced souls will quite regularly underestimate the amount of energy they are going to need for incarnation, sometimes even ignoring the advice of their elders in the matter. Why would this happen? One answer is that the higher the level of energy left behind, the more active it is able to be in the light realms. Not only can it continue to mix with other members of its soul group but also if the energy is high enough, it can continue with various other aspects of learning and experience in the light realms. Thus speeding up soul development.

There is another aspect which none of the pioneers have identified. Souls can also select the levels of specific emotions they have been working with previously that they want to bring into incarnation again. They can also choose to take particular past-life strengths with them as well, in order to help them to face specific trials. All of the energy level and specific past-life emotions and strengths come together in a complex interplay. Sometimes subjects report that it has been worked out for them as a 'package'. When they do have an involvement in their selection, they usually discuss their options with their spirit guide before their elders review their choice.

With his elders Liam Thompson reports that he will be taking seventy-five percent of his soul energy. Assuming he is a reasonably experienced soul because he is almost at guide level, this shows just how much help is needed to break his current repetitive suicide pattern:

What level of soul energy will you be taking down with you in this life?
A lot. Seventy percent, seventy-five percent. I always take too little.
How's that going to help you in this life?
It'll help me recognize my intuition properly. Help me gain a better

strength of self. My spirit guide will be there to help. I need to be calm and centered and the feelings will come.

The narrative then moves on to the emotions he is taking that have been decided for him:

Are there any negative emotions that you're taking from past lives?
Anger.
And what percentage are you taking?
Only a small amount. It's under the surface. Something that's got to be worked on.
Are there any other negative emotions you're taking with you?
Envy. It's been from a number of lives.
In your last life you had plenty of resentment. Are you taking any of that with you into this life?
Hmm. Not really because my mum and dad in this life are not my mum and dad from that previous one.
Did you have any choices about these negative emotions you're taking forward?
They've been worked out for me. I have to work on these.

Jack Hammond also faces a difficult life with the Maori gene to help him overcome his repetitive problem of being a loner. Previously he had ignored advice given to him and not taken enough soul energy with him in last life. So it is not a surprise when he takes a high proportion of his soul energy at a level of 80%. He also reports that the twenty percent of his soul energy that remains in the light realms will still be reasonably active. This extends to him being able to return the complement of the joke his soul mates played on him on his return:

I didn't take enough last time.

Was this your choice?

It was my choice, and I've been arrogant before. Maybe I was thinking I was more enlightened than I was.

What percentage do you finally agree to take down?

Eighty percent.

And what does Garth think about that?

He's nodding his head.

The twenty percent that remains, what's it going to be doing?

I'll be part of the welcoming committee, or greeting group and there for meeting people coming back, [Laughs] and to play jokes! Um, but there's learning to be done. Twenty percent is strong enough to do learning.

So what learning will you be doing?

Research, but it might be pretty low-key stuff.

Liz Kendry too needs to break a repetitive cycle, which for her is one of dependence on her soul partner Charles. After detailed discussions with her spirit guide, she accepts the advice of her elders. She should slightly increase the percentage of certain emotions such as sadness and loneliness that she is working on, because she will be better prepared to deal with them this time. However this comes with the advice to increase the soul energy she should take from seventy-five to eighty percent. She also provides an excellent overview of why the elders are in a rather better position to judge the energy she will require:

> What I don't know completely is the other lives that are going to interact with mine... They see the whole picture. They see the other souls' interactions with mine, and the other challenges I may have and the choices I may have to make. How if I make one choice over another and it leads me down a different path I may need more energy that way.

Meanwhile, Liz too describes how the twenty percent of her energy that remains behind in the light realms can continue to learn, at least in a modest way:

> I can still work on some of the emotions and some of the lessons I have to learn that may not be as significant as the ones I have to learn on earth. So I pick some of the minor ones to have a look at.

Given her description of her soul group that is working with the energy matrix that surrounds the earth, it can be assumed that Laura Harper may be a reasonably experienced soul who will require a rather lower percentage of her energy. This is indeed what happens. She too commences the selection process by having a detailed discussion with her guide. It soon becomes clear that there is a compromise between her trying to complete her emotional learning while incarnate, and at the same time trying to leave plenty of soul energy behind to continue her energy work in the light realms:

> *Do you discuss what percentage of emotions from those past lives you're going to take?*
> Yes. I'm feeling very strongly that I'm going to take more than she recommends.
> *How much are you going to take?*
> Unfinished emotions? I'm going to take almost all of it. Ninety-five percent.
> *What does your guide say?*
> She's shaking her head. She's saying that will be very challenging, but she says she'll help, and stay close.
> *By taking that ninety-five percent does that mean you can clear all these emotions out of the way in one lifetime?*
> That's what I'm determined to do. I feel as if I've been dragging them around like a great ball and chain and it's time to free myself.

Do you have a discussion about the level of soul energy you're going to take down with you?

I don't know why. Why am I wanting to take so little?

How much are you going to take down?

Thirty-five percent.

What does your guide say about that?

She says I'm mad.

Is this going to make it a very difficult life?

She shakes her head a bit, like 'gosh'.

What figure does she suggest?

She thinks I should take sixty.

And what's your final decision?

I'm just asking myself why I want to take so little. The answer is because I want to do so much more. I want to learn so much more about this light transmission up here. I feel like I'm trying to do so much. I've decided that I can up it to forty-five.

She then finds out what her elders, who she calls wise ones, think about these choices:

They're reminding me that it'll take me a lot longer to do the work on my emotions if I take so little energy. They really understand what I want to do, to work hard on both realms. They're just reminding me about gentleness, and lightness, and rest. They're also reminding me about all the help that's available from them, and from Iscanara.

Turning now to past-life strengths, having chosen to take seventy percent soul energy because it felt right, Katja Eisler reports that she also takes down a kind of soldier consciousness to protect her:

What emotions do you take from past lives?

A tendency for violence, and to fight.

What percentage of these emotions do you bring down?

Forty percent.

What's the purpose of bringing this?

To protect me, like a kind of soldier consciousness. It's not violence. It's more of a force, a forward-moving force. It's active and strategy-oriented, goal-oriented accompanied by very high alertness.

Veronica Perry illustrates the factors that have to be considered before her traumatic past life as an orphan. The selection process begins with a negotiation with her elders about her soul energy:

I'm sort of negotiating. I feel I want to take as much energy as possible because I think I will need it.

What figure are you thinking of?

I want to take ninety percent.

And what do the elders say to you about that?

They're not happy with that.

What do they suggest?

They feel if I take that amount of energy there wouldn't be any margin for losing any.

Would you be able to continue any activities in the spirit realms?

No, I'd be quite weakened.

What figure are the elders suggesting?

They're suggesting fifty percent.

And what figure do you finally decide on?

Fifty-five percent.

Given the nature of the past life she will face, it may seem strange that the elders do not recommend a higher figure. Veronica's explanation for this is as follows:

Our group needs a certain amount of energy to be held and maintained in the spirit realms, so that it can be drawn upon by any member in times of need. Sometimes this will manifest as a spirit helper or guide, and sometimes by absently sending some energy.

This is an important point not covered by others. Even after splitting the soul energy for incarnation, the life plan can allow for a top up in an emergency. It also illustrates how the elders are in a better position to judge the split of soul energy by considering the wider aspects, such as the requirements of the soul group. Veronica also indicates that the individual link is important as well:

I won't be able to meditate in that life but whilst I'm asleep and dreaming my soul energy will be able to communicate with my subconscious as in any other life. It will be able to remind me of the peace and the love, so that I can carry on with that life until its proper finishing point.

Veronica will be facing a difficult life as an orphan for altruistic purposes rather than for her own learning, so it is understandable why all this extra help is being offered. As the narrative continues it will come as no surprise that she will not be taking any negative emotions to work on, only the strengths of peace and love from a previous past-life:

This is going to be a very short life. I'm being offered positive past-life energy to take with me.
What energy can you bring with you?
Inner peace from the last life.
What percentage can you bring with you?
I can bring all of that with me.
Is there any other positive energy you can take?

The love I felt in that life as well.

What percentage of that can you take?

I can take as much as I want.

What figure are you thinking of?

I want to leave some of that here to be shared. To share with my group, but I want to take half of it with me because I have my inner peace.

Will you be taking any unfinished negative energy with you?

No. There'll be enough to collect.

Embarkation and Relayering

The subjects are now ready to embark on their journey back into the physical realm. Katja Eisler describes the experience being like: 'A long tunnel that's getting darker at the end'. Jack Hammond reports as follows:

The word 'chute' comes to mind, but it's not like any chute I know. If I was going to be clichéd about it, it's like I'm going to be put in place and rocketed off.

Liam Thompson also senses that his return is extremely quick:

I go to like a sedation center. Not so much sedated, but I have to wait until it's the right time to go. This is a place where I can be alone with my thoughts before I'm ready to leave... Then it's fast, it's quick, and I'm there. It's almost instantaneous.

However the most detailed reports come from three of the subjects with minimal prior knowledge. Veronica Perry opens by describing how she is in a holding chamber:

I don't have much time here this time. I'm going to incarnate again.

How does it work?

My spirit guide comes to get me and we go to another chamber.

Just describe this chamber.

It's a holding chamber. It's a circular chamber. The best word I can think of to describe it is like a… it's almost like an airport. It's like there are lots of different gates or openings to go through.

Whereabouts do you go in this chamber?

My guide is showing me. There's some others of my soul group here as well. I'm going to the left of the chamber. They're incarnating as well. I think we're going to be doing some work together in this life.

How do you know when it's time to leave this chamber and to start the process of incarnating?

We're all leaving the chamber together. Although some of my soul group will be born physically before me, we all leave at the same time. The timing here is not an issue. We'll all arrive at the appropriate time for our lives to start on earth.

This idea that the timing of their departure is not an issue needs to be examined. Time does not have the same meaning in the spirit realms as it does in our physical lives. Without the constraints of a physical body that decays, soul energy in spirit realms can move to any future period in Earth time without any sense of time delay. This explains the apparent contradictions that can arise when different timings of incarnation with family and friends might span generations.

Another important part of this process is to pick up the past-life emotions and experiences that will be needed for the new incarnation. The name that's been given to this is 're-layer-ing', and this is an aspect not mentioned by any of the interlife pioneers. The process is the opposite to 'delayering' that was discussed as part of the healing before entering the spirit realms.

This is Veronica's description of how she moves through different layers picking up the past-life emotions and experiences she will need on her departure from them. Her description of becoming lighter and brighter during this process seems to be the opposite of what we would expect but it's her way of describing the process of gathering the energies she needs. Finally she describes the experience of her soul energy splitting:

Tell me what you experience between leaving with your soul group and actually merging with the physical body?
I feel that my soul is working through different levels of energy and different phases to pick up the different energies that it's been agreed that I take with me. I'm sort of drawing those in as I move through the different stages.
Ok, just describe in detail how that works and what you experience?
All of the resources that I have available to me are there and I expand my energy to envelope them and draw them into me and each resource I draw in makes me feel lighter and brighter.
How do you know what resources to draw in?
It happens. I suppose it is intuitive, drawing them in. They've been made available to me, I don't have to go and get them. They're just available, and I can just expand to bring them into me.
Have you actually split your soul-energy yet?
No.
Go to that point and describe how it happens?
I can feel it from two different angles at this point. The persona of the physical incarnation that I'm about to have is being drawn into part of my soul energy, and that part of my soul energy is being released by the part that is staying behind. I can feel myself as soul energy releasing that other part and pushing it forwards to incarnation. I can also feel the soul energy that has taken on the new life

being pushed forwards by the rest of my soul energy. It's very calm and it's very accepting.

Veronica is not alone in providing a description of the relayering process. Wendy Simpson seems to refer to it briefly:

> I get the feeling of going somewhere else before coming back. There is a place where people's energy form changes back to normal physical form… There are other souls here… We've all got to come back… It feels like there is a cloak being put on me. I'm saying goodbye, although knowing that it is not going to be forever.

Nicola Barnard goes into even more detail on relayering, and with a real sense that she is re-experiencing it:

> *Tell me what happens next?*
> I need to get all these layers. It's like this feeling of needing to get dressed.
> *How do you go about this?*
> Each layer feels like it's a subtle energy. There's nothing solid or material about it, individually they are almost transparent, but cumulatively they create the impression of the material.
> *Where do you get this energy from?*
> It's like the layers are hanging in the air and I can get another one and another one, and so on, and with each one I get more of a sense of who I am.
> *Is the energy collected for you?*
> They are there already. It's like a suit. I'm experiencing some changes in terms of not being light any more. Some of this is not very helpful, or nice. It's a bit like putting on wet clothes. It's just the odd layer I don't feel so comfortable with but I've chosen

them.

What's happening to you now?

I'm in the process of taking this stuff on. There's like this gauze material that passes through my energy body, and on its own it wouldn't do anything, but in conjunction with the other layers it's beginning to build a sense of this new being I'm coming into. It feels like the energy has to be quite dense to be able to incarnate, that there have to be quite a lot of these layers.

Merging with the Body

It is often reported that souls feel the full harsh reality of being back in the physical at the point of birth, and that while in the womb they are more protected. Despite a certain initial reluctance to enter the baby, this is the impression given by Nicola Barnard as she continues following her relayering:

I don't really want to go.

Whereabouts are you at the moment?

I'm still up, and I'm not quite certain. I've chosen this but [Big sigh] I have a job to do.

What happens next?

They want another baby. There's some kind of agreement for me to be there. Around about conception time there's this subtle acceptance. They know my energy, not consciously, but their higher self and my higher self agree how it's going to be.

Go to the point when you join the baby.

I'm in the womb. It's dark.

How many months into pregnancy is it?

It's got a sense of being a baby, with arms and legs. It's not so late, I'd say about three or four months.

Whereabouts do you enter?

The head.

And what do you experience as you enter?
I'm aware that I've done it before. I'm not too phased by it. It seems quite calm and peaceful, and there's a sense of it being right, you know?

Newton reports that the process of merging the soul with the physical brain of the baby is not easy, and must be undertaken gradually. Of course the emotional state of the mother affects the baby, particularly negative emotions. So the soul may have to wait for these to change or loosen up the mother's energy patterns before entry. The soul also needs to adjust its vibrations to those of the baby's mind so frequently it will float in and out over a period of a few months. Wendy Simpson reports that she feels confined when she first enters the baby at seven weeks into the pregnancy, but she can 'go in and out' until about three months. Katja Eisler confirms this idea and also is aware of the mother's emotions:

How old is this baby from the point of conception?
Six months.
What happens?
I take a moment, and watch it.
What part of the body do you enter?
Through the brain.
What does it feel like?
There's a lot of energy there. I can't help feeling a little bit trapped. I'm floating a little bit in and out.
When do you finally merge with the baby?
Eight months.
What does that feel like?
I can feel the difficulties my mother has with being pregnant, the disappointment, she feels she is too young and it's the wrong man. She fell in love with another man.

How long does the merger take?

It happens over a period of time. I have to get used to the brain, it's not an easy brain. It feels like my soul is much softer and quieter than the brain of this baby.

Unfortunately Katja was not the only subject to experience coming into a less than happy environment. Jack Hammond knows he will have a difficult time once his Maori gene is discovered, but he has a surprise to find the initial environment in the womb is unwelcoming:

It's like I'm only observing, I'm not really in the baby yet... It's almost like I am waiting to see if it is going to be ok... I join about two or three months [from conception]... It's not a happy time to have been conceived. My mum is alone, and she's crying a lot. It's a bad start.

Liam Thompson also finds the experience somewhat uncomfortable, although it appears this has nothing to do with his mother:

I merge with the baby smoothly... It is four months [from conception]. He's coming out early... First I connect with the brain. That's the hardest part... I spread myself over and around it. There's nothing there yet. It's like going into a room and turning on the light... To be back in a human body again feels disturbing, cold and dense.

Like Nicola, Lene Haugland is not keen to enter the baby. Unlike the majority of subjects who report that they come in via the head or brain, she does so via the throat:

I don't want to join... I'm just hanging around, I don't like this situation. The baby is two months [from conception]... I have to enter before it's three months old, because I need to connect the soul to the physical body... I enter via the throat... It's like I've penetrated it with some color. It was meant to be that I penetrate the throat, it's very important for this child... It was the only part of the body that had color, vibrational color. It was blue.

Most of the subjects report that they enter between two and four months into the pregnancy, with only Katja leaving her initial entry until six months. However Veronica Perry comes in later still. We find that the start to her life as an orphan is both unexpected and intensely traumatic:

Go to that point just before you merge with the baby and tell me what you experience.
Great confusion. I suddenly feel very heavy. My energy's merging with the physical. It's quite painful.
How does this compare with other times?
Sometimes it's easier than this. It depends what stage the baby is at.
How many months from conception is the baby?
Seven.
Have you ever incarnated this late before?
No. Usually I am able to join the baby before this, and to move in and out before joining fully.
What's the reason for joining at seven months in this particular baby?
Oh. There was another soul here before.
And what happened to that other soul?
There were two souls here before me. There was another baby. This was supposed to be two babies.
Did something happen to the other baby?
[Deep sigh] It was aborted.
At this point Veronica breaks into heavy sobbing, proving once again

just how intense regression recall can be. After being calmed and reassured she is regressed back to the interlife to investigate further what had been happening in the womb. Now it becomes abundantly clear why she was so traumatized:

In that life I chose to be born into a world where children were abused and unwanted. The soul that had chosen to go through into that life before me was so traumatized by the other twin baby being aborted that they opted out as well. So what I felt on joining the surviving baby was the shock and the sadness of that previous soul. They'd left that energy behind. That's another reason why I was allowed to take so much soul energy with me, and so many resources.

The Veil of Amnesia

The onset of amnesia about the light realms is commonly understood to be a crucial process that allows us to operate effectively in the physical realm. With too much recall of the ecstasy and purity of our true spiritual home most people would probably be overcome by homesickness and the desire to go back could be too strong. Another reason is that knowing all about our life plan would be like taking an exam when all the answers are known.

For Nicola Barnard this process commenced even as she was leaving the light realms, and it seems likely that this is an automatic part of relayering. It also appears that this is not a sudden but a gradual process, so that there is some flexibility about exactly when the full memory blocks finally come into play. At the point of joining the narrative she starts to whisper to herself for a short while. This is not uncommon in interlife sessions as subjects attempt to understand what they are experiencing and how they can formulate it into words. She then starts to describe how her memory seems to be fading, although she seems to be resisting the process:

[Whispers to herself] I'm forgetting. I think I must be going because it's becoming difficult to remember where I've come from.

What's happening?

With these new layers, it's as if the truth is gradually being wiped away. I want to remember my soul family, but I don't know if I will. I've forgotten so many times.

What happens next?

It's time to go down. I know that it's chosen, but I don't feel excited. Everything, all the details have been taken care of. It seems very clear where to go and what to do, it's just not so easy to leave. The more layers of experience that came in, the less connected I was with the other reality anyway.

Katja Eisler reports that for her amnesia occurred early, around birth. Lene Haugland felt it was delayed, until the baby was around seven months old. This could support the common idea that one of the reasons small babies spend a great deal of time sleeping is because they are still able to remember some aspects of being in the light realms. Liam Thompson suggests that the process will not be complete until somewhat later in his childhood:

> *At what point are the memory blocks going to be put into place?*
> As a child.
> *And how does the process of putting these memory blocks into place work?*
> As my brain develops its personality, my immortal self will quieten down like a light bulb switching off. It's never completely out, it's always there, always on dim.

Of course Liam reminds us that even with amnesia we can still contact our core soul energy, our higher self, while in our physical lives.

9

CONCLUSION

What is a good man but a bad man's teacher.
What is a bad man but a good man's job.
If you don't understand this,
you get lost however intelligent you are.
It is the great secret.
Lao-Tzu, Chinese Taoist Master.

Guidance and Support

One of the most important practical implications of this research is that help from the light realms is far more readily available than many people realize. When Liam Thompson goes back to his elders for a real time progress review they advise him of the methods that can be used to contact our spirit guide and other helpers:

> It will come through dreams, or a deep inner knowing... I need to be emotionless to get divine guidance... They tell me to look within myself, that I have all the answers in the world, and that any situation that exists can be healed. They tell me to trust... They also say that meditation will be very helpful, but I have to persevere, nothing comes easy... Every day, for ten minutes at least... Also, my spirit guide will be there to help... I just need to be calm, and centered, and the feelings will come.

It is interesting that Katja Eisler's spirit guide confirms the advice given to Liam about the importance of meditating for a minimum of ten minutes every day:

He says 'just call me'... It's more powerful in meditation, and you should do this while sitting and not lying down, otherwise you go too deep. He says every day, for ten minutes, is fine... He also says I can do it any time. I can just call him by name, or picture his appearance in my mind.

The insistence that we can get help at any time just by asking for it, is also confirmed by Jack Hammond's spirit guide Garth:

Oh! I've been admonished! I've been told 'remember to ask for help'... I should meditate and go to a quiet place to bring Garth's presence, and ask. Oh! You can just ask straight out because there'll be times when you can't go away and lie down, or find a quiet place. Then you can just ask, straight off.

Meanwhile Lisbet Halvorsen makes the intriguing and not unrelated insight during her interlife that she should continue to make plans with her soul group while incarnate and asleep:

It seems as if I go in and out of this group in this life, maybe when I'm sleeping... It seems as if it's going on right now, in parallel. So it seems like I go there, and we plan things, and I get support and comfort and then I go down again.

Subject Feedback

Although interlife research helps to build a proper framework to understand about the soul memories between lives, equally crucial is the personal impact it has on those who experience it. Between about three months and one year after their interlife session the subjects where asked to provide feedback. A selection of these shows a moving testimony in their own words, of the profound change it brought into their current life. Nadine Castelle was brief but to the point:

The experience has propelled me to another level. It was a wonderful gift.

Lene Haugland was similarly brief but upbeat:

My life has changed a lot since the session. All the fear I had has gone, and I have never felt so safe in myself, and so loved. I will always be grateful for that.

Katja Eisler was equally grateful and felt it had helped her in many ways including her difficult relationship with her mother:

My interlife session helped me in many ways. It has opened up my view even further about the greater meaning and sense of life. It has helped me to see people in a different way to see that we are all in this together, and have a lot of learning experiences together. To see that we choose lessons for a lifetime, and our parents as well. This has helped me a lot, because my relationship with my mother was always very difficult, but now I can see it more as a chance for growth. I also felt more connected after the sessions, and I lost my fear of death. Not completely, but a great deal. I have started to have more compassion for myself, and to understand a lot of feelings and thoughts better than before.

Wendy Simpson referred specifically to the healing for her disabling ME. Short for Myalgic Encephalomy, it causes aches and prolonged tiredness. Her life purpose is the way she treats others, which was deliberately made difficult by having to overcome her low energy levels. She discovered from the elders that the ME had now fulfilled its earlier karmic purpose and was no longer needed:

My interlife session has been a great help to me, firstly, my attitude to life has seemed to change and I seem to have released any fears about death. I have become more 'laid-back' about life and more interested in looking at the qualities of my personality. My illness has much improved and my energy levels have greatly increased. I have a very positive attitude towards my future and life purpose and have been taking active constructive steps to make changes in my life. The whole experience was very special and totally amazing and very profound. I am very grateful for the opportunity to have had this session and experience and the healing that came through.

Meanwhile, Liz Kendry provided this most heart-warming description of how her session had helped her to cope with the loss of her husband, Charles:

Since the session I've been able to rationalize the loss of my husband, and have been able to move through the grieving process quicker, knowing that he still exists and that we will meet up again. It has also enabled me to get on with life and not get stuck wallowing in self-pity for what I have lost. Something that I had clearly done in previous lives. By getting on with life, I don't mean that I have run out and found a replacement for my husband, I would never do that. However, I can continue with life and enjoy it knowing that it is one of my life lessons to manage and live a full life without him. Occasionally I say to myself 'what were we thinking to have planned this?' However, I have accepted that we did make this decision, and I have to live out the rest of the plan. Not that I know entirely what the plan is, besides independence. Knowing that we continue after death has helped me lead a more positive life, and I am now more conscious of the decisions I make and how they impact others.

One of the most crucial insights to be gained from the interlife which both Katja and Liz emphasized is:

> When we are facing challenging circumstances, it helps to remember that almost certainly we chose them to help us to learn and grow.

Turning finally now to Veronica Perry, whose detailed sessions and lack of prior knowledge made such an important contribution to the research:

> Although I feel that my words cannot do it justice, this was for me an extremely profound experience. It put a lot of 'issues' in my life into context, and enabled me to look at the bigger picture in terms of the journey of my energetic soul. I can only say thank you to the universe for making this opportunity available, for giving me this glimpse of my soul, my life between lives. It was a magical, wonderful and humbling experience. It has touched me, changed my view on life, and opened up my eyes, my heart and my soul to a greater calm. I have understanding, love and respect for life, for others on their journeys, for the universe, and for myself.

Final Thoughts

Hopefully from this selection of subject feedback it has been possible to convey something of the profound and awe-inspiring experience that awaits all of us when we return to our true spiritual home. It also shows the profound healing and spiritual growth that can come from integrating an interlife session into a person's current life. Over time this will be recognized and understood as a powerful psychological tool.

The research of this book has been built on the superb work of the interlife pioneers, and Michael Newton in particular. Clearly there are some areas where interpretations differ. An important one is the emphasis on the fluidity of the experience, despite the underlying consistency of its elements. Yet some differences are surely to be expected from any attempt to expand understanding of such a crucial area of research. Nor does this take anything away from the huge respect for all of the pioneers.

At this point it would be useful to return to the issue of prior knowledge, and to re-emphasize the deliberate selection policy. One third of the subjects had a fairly high degree of prior knowledge of interlife books, particularly Newton's work. Another third had had at least some exposure to it. The final third had minimal or no exposure at all. Yet the consistent underlying elements of the experience are there for all. Not only that but Lene Haugland, who did have some prior knowledge, provided the following important insights in her subsequent feedback:

During and after my session I knew only one thing. My experience was not what I had expected. Most of it was totally new to me. When I was in that 'state of mind' I couldn't choose what I was going to see or feel, and anything I had learned or heard about before didn't matter. I can remember that my mind was trying to tell me many times that some of the things that I experienced had to be wrong, because I had never heard or read about them before. So I know that my experience was totally mine.

Finally, what better way to close the book than with the further insights of Veronica Perry about the gift of life on earth, which came during her final progress evaluation with her elders:

At a soul level I've always enjoyed my lives. Even though some have been hard, and there's been a lot of pain from things I've seen and done. Whenever I go back to soul I appreciate it. I appreciate all these opportunities I've been given to learn, and to teach on occasions, and to understand all the different range of emotions and feelings we can have here. Yes, there are painful things to feel and to experience, but there are also wonderful things to feel and experience too. Just the feeling of sunshine, the feeling of the breeze, the smells, just the happiness of being able to walk in a meadow. These are all things that I feel at a soul level.

APPENDIX

The History of Interlife Research

If the pioneering therapists were surprised by the results of their research into past lives, imagine the added surprise when several of them independently discovered that their clients could recall details of their time between lives as well. All of a sudden, ordinary people with no particular religious or spiritual background began to deliver profound insights into the interlife experience. Even more impressive was that their revelations proved to be highly consistent.

Joel Whitton's experience was typical of the early pioneers. He gave an imprecise command to a client in the middle of a past life regression. The instruction was to go back to the 'life' before the one she had just been regressed into. He was amazed to find her describing herself as 'in the sky... waiting to be born... watching my mother'. Following this he made a huge contribution to the understanding of the interlife experience by investigating the phenomenon with some of his more responsive clients. This was published in 1986 with Joe Fisher in *Life Between Life*.

In contrast Helen Wambach deliberately instigated a research program in which she regressed volunteers in groups. She had already achieved success in gathering the first real statistical data about past lives using this method. 750 of her volunteers were regressed back to the time before they were born in this life and asked whether they chose to return, whether anyone helped them in their decision, and how they felt about coming back. Her results published in 1979 in *Life Before Life* were impressive. At the same time Peter Ramster was working with past lives and also made some important discoveries about the interlife that were incorporated into *The Truth About Reincarnation*.

Over the next decade three more interlife pioneers came to the fore, all in America. Dolores Cannon stumbled upon it again by accident when a subject died in a past life and then began describing how they were 'floating above their body', and her further research was published in 1993 in *Between Death and Life*. Another was the controversial book by Shakuntala Modi that includes her views on demonic possession, something that most of the other pioneers dismiss. However the book *Remarkable Healings* does contains some highly consistent summaries of her findings about the interlife.

Michael Newton was the first pioneer to successfully bring interlife research into the public consciousness. He was skeptical about past life regression in the 1960's after working a number of years in traditional hypnotherapy. He began to appreciate its capabilities when a subject was directed to go to the source of a pain in his right side and described being stabbed as a soldier in WWI. His persistent pain was immediately and permanently relieved. Not long after this he also stumbled upon the interlife by accident when issuing an imprecise command to another subject who was particularly receptive to entering deeper states of hypnotic trance. During the 1970's and 1980's he quietly concentrated most of his efforts on investigating the interlife as thoroughly as he could with a great many cases before he was satisfied with his own mapping of the spirit world relating to soul activity between lives. Finally, he published the most detailed interlife account of any of the pioneers in *Journey of Souls* in 1994 and later with *Destiny of Souls* in 2000.

Research Details

The spread of the number of elders in the council reported by those subjects who met with them is summarized in the following table:

NO. ELDERS	NO. SUBJECTS	
1 to 5	8	67%
6 to 10	3	25%
11 to 15	1	8%

The spread of the number of souls in the soul group reported by the subjects is summarized in the following table:

NO. SOULS	NO. SUBJECTS	
1 to 5	2	15%
6 to 10	5	38%
11 to 15	4	31%
16 to 20	1	8%
21 to 30	1	8%

Each subject is given a pseudonym, but the other information about the subject has been carefully recorded.

The classifications of the subject's prior knowledge of the interlife experience before their session is as follows:

- *High* – They had previously read about the interlife in some detail, and had retained a significant amount of that information.
- *Medium* – They had previously read about the interlife, often some years ago and had forgotten the details.
- *Low* – They had not previously heard or read about the interlife, or had very limited prior exposure.
- The numbers in bold indicate the element that has been included in the book. The other numbers indicate simply that the subject

experienced it.

- The numbering reflects the order in which the elements were recalled during the session. Where a subject was effectively combining multiple elements at once, they are shown as (a), (b) and so on. Where a subject returned to an element more than once at different times, it is given multiple numbers.

- Veronica Perry's second interlife only covered the transition and healing elements.

PERSONAL DETAILS

SUBJECT	Age	M/F	Country	Prior Know	Transition	Healing	Guide Review	Elder Review	Soul group
Nicola Barnard	30s	F	UK	L	**1**	**2**		3	
Magnus Bergen	20s	M	Norway	L	1	**2**	**4**	5a	**3**
Nadine Castelle	30s	F	UK	M	1	**2**	**4a**		**3 6 8**
Katja Eisler	30s	F	Germany	M	1	**5**	2	3	**4 6**
Lisbet Halvorsen	20s	F	Norway	M	1a	2	**1b**		**3 5**
Laura Harper	40s	F	UK	H	1	**2**		**4**	3a
Lene Haugland	40s	F	Norway	M	**1**	2 4 6			**5a**
Jack Hammond	50s	M	NZ	H	**1**			2	**3**
Liz Kendry	30s	F	Canada	M	**1**	2	**4**	**5**	**3 6**
Marta Petersen	20s	F	Denmark	H	**1**		**3**		2
Veronica Perry 1	30s	F	UK	L	**1**	**2**	**4**		3, 7
Veronica Perry 2	30s	F	UK	L	**1**	**2**			
David Stephens	30s	M	UK	H	1	**2**			
Liam Thompson	20s	M	UK	H	**1**	**3 7**	**2 5**		**4**
Wendy Simpson	40s	F	UK	L	**1**	3		**2**	**4**

PERSONAL DETAILS

SUBJECT	Age	M/F	Country	Prior Know	Special activity	Plan w group	Life preview	Life choice	Plan w. elders
Nicola Barnard	30s	F	UK	L			4b		4a
Magnus Bergen	20s	M	Norway	L					5b
Nadine Castelle	30s	F	UK	M	5 9			4b	7
Katja Eisler	30s	F	Germany	M				7a	
Lisbet Halvorsen	20s	F	Norway	M	4			6	
Laura Harper	40s	F	UK	H	3b			5a	6a
Lene Haugland	40s	F	Norway	M	3 5b		7		
Jack Hammond	50s	M	NZ	H			4a		
Liz Kendry	30s	F	Canada	M		7		8	10a
Marta Petersen	20s	F	Denmark	H	4			6	5
Veronica Perry 1	30s	F	UK	L			5	6a	
Veronica Perry 2	30s	F	UK	L					
David Stephens	30s	M	UK	H			3	4	
Liam Thompson	20s	M	UK	H	6	9	10		8a
Wendy Simpson	40s	F	UK	L			5	6	

Questions Used for the Subject Feedback

1. Before your session how much awareness did you have of the life between lives, called the interlife? Had you read any of Michael Newton's books, or any other books that mentioned the interlife, or discussed it with anyone else that had? If so, do you think it consciously affected your session in any way?

2. In what ways has your life changed following your interlife session that you think was directly attributable to it?

Comparison with Other Interlife Pioneers

This grid shows the major elements of an interlife that have been covered in other interlife pioneer's books, based on an analysis from the *Book of the Soul* by Ian Lawton.

	This book	New-ton	Ramp-ster	Whitt-on	Cannon	Modi	Fiore
Transition via a tunnel or light	•	•	•	•	•	•	•
Met by friends, family or spirit guide	•	•	•	•	•	•	•
Varied perception of surrounding	•	•		•	•		
Intial rest and energy restoring	•	•	•			•	
Healing shower of energy	•	•			•	•	
Delayering as part of energy healing	•						
Rehabilitation for traumatized souls	•	•			•		
Soul group members at similar level	•	•	•	•	•	•	
Review with elders	•	•		•	•	•	•

Replay/role-play via life books and films	•	•	•	•	•	•	
Ongoing classroom learning	•	•	•	•	•	•	
Non judgmental nature of reviews	•	•	•	•	•	•	•
Next life planning	•	•	•	•	•	•	•
Choice to reject the life plan offered	•	•	•	•	•	•	•
Multiple life plans offered	•	•	•				
Training in specialization	•	•		•	•		
Relayering as part of reincarnation	•						

GLOSSARY

Altruistic Life: A life that a soul deliberately chooses to be of service to others. Such lives are not planned for the learning of the soul themselves but for those around them. It is sometimes called a filler life.

Astral Realm: The dimension closely linked to the physical world in which the spiritual body normally passes through, and in which trapped spirits reside.

Attachments: These are the trapped soul energies that after death have attached themselves to an incarnate person, place or object rather than returning to the light realms. They will however be reunited with their core soul energy at some point.

Body Traumas: The physical wounds from past life traumas that are carried over by the soul but are not healed in the spirit realms. They can be strongly imprinted on the next life physical body.

Core Soul Energy: It's sometimes called our 'higher self' and is that portion of soul energy left behind in the light realms when a soul reincarnates. This energy will be more active or dormant depending on what proportion of the total it represents.

Council of Elders: A collective name for a group of elders.

Delayering: A new term to describe the automatic process of healing and energy lightening that all souls must receive in order to make the transition to the light realms.

Elders: The wise and experienced souls who assist those still incarnating with a past-life review and next-life planning advice. They work at a higher level than spirit guides. Clients call them a variety of names such as Elders, Wise Ones, Higher Ones, Masters or Council.

Emotional Lessons: This is an emotion that a soul is attempting to master by experiencing it in a physical form on earth. Members of the same soul group often work on the same lesson together.

Fluidity: Interlife sessions vary in their order of events, how extensively any event is experienced and also the frequency such as the number of visits to see the elders.

Karma: The traditional ideas of karma as a process of 'action and reaction', 'paying off debts' or 'reaping what you sow' are very simplistic. Through interlife evidence it is seen as a process of soul learning, experience, and growth often through difficult life situations.

Holographic Soul: The soul splits for reincarnation and both parts retain a link to keep the soul memories for the whole soul.

Interlife: The experience of soul memories between lives in the light realms. This is also known as the life between lives.

Life Between Lives: The experience of soul memories between lives in the light realms. This is also known as interlife.

Life Path: The most probable course of any life if that person makes the decisions that they have planned in the light realms. The soul may also have agreed certain triggers that are intended to prompt them to stay on that path.

Life Previews: The foretaste of the next life received in the light realms, which represents the major probabilities for that life.

Light Realm: The true home of all soul energies, and the realm most closely connected with the Source itself.

Next-Life Planning: The whole process of planning discussions with elders, spirit guides and soul mates.

Past-Life Review: The process of reviewing and learning from the last incarnate life. It involves an element of discussion with elders, spirit guides and soul mates.

Regression: The process by which a client enters an altered state of awareness so that they can recall past lives or the interlife. This is usually achieved by hypnosis, but other methods can be used.

Relayering: A new term to describe the process of collecting the emotions and energies that a soul wants to work with in the next incarnate life.

Secondary Soul Groups: Souls often work with other souls other than their soul mates. These groups are formed for planning for a particular life, and the members often have different soul colors.

Source: The ultimate source of everything and the creation of the universe, and what our individual soul consciousness is connected with. Sometimes it's called the Oneness and various religions have other names.

Soul: The spiritual energy that contains all of a person's past life experiences and learnings.

Soul Color: The energy of each soul has a color. This changes as souls grow to become more experienced and evolved. In the spirit realms soul mates often have the same color.

Soul Energy Reintegration: The process by which the returning soul energy is reunited with the core soul energy left behind in the light realms.

Soul Fragmentation: Following intense emotional interactions incarnate souls can lose fragments of their energy to others.

Soul Groups: Groups of soul mates that work closely together both in the light realms and in successions of lives in the physical realm.

Soul Mates: The other members of a soul group who work closely together both in the light realms and in successions of lives in the physical realm.

Specialist Skills: Specific skills, such as teaching, guiding, healing, energy work that souls increasingly train in as they become more experienced. A soul group can come together to work on particular skills just as it can to work on emotional lessons.

Spirit Guide: Specialist souls who oversee the life plan of those that are incarnate. They provide guidance and advice during past-life review and next-life planning.

Spirit Realms: Another term for the light realms often used by regression subjects.

Spiritual Regression; The process of guiding a person to the soul's memories between lives. This is also known as the life between lives, or interlife regression.

Spirits of Light: A general term for any soul in the spirit realms.

Trapped Soul Energies/Spirits: Spirits that after death fail to recognize that they are dead or remain attached to the physical realm. They remain trapped in the astral realm, and can form an attachment to an incarnate person or place.

Triggers: Emotional or even physical reminders implanted in the light realms for the incarnate person to recognize that there is an emotional lesson to be worked on, or a choice to be made that is relevant to their life path.

Veil of Amnesia: The process by which a reincarnating soul gradually loses its memory of the light realms and the life planning. The aim is to prevent us feeling homesickness, and not 'taking an exam knowing all the answers in advance'. It may not be completed until early childhood.

Wise Ones: A term some souls use instead of elders. It can mean souls who operate at a higher level.

SOURCE REFERENCES

Although most of the professionals quoted in the book have doctorates in psychology or psychiatry, I do not use the title 'Dr' throughout the book. This is not intended to be disrespectful, but to avoid laborious repetition. The bibliography contains further book details.

INTRODUCTION

Lawton, *The Book of the Soul*: analysis of interlife pioneers, chapter 5, pp122

Stevenson, Ian, *Twenty Case of Suggested Reincarnation:* detailed analysis of 20 children who remembered past lives, Swarnata Mishra case, chapter 2, pp.67-91.

Stevenson, Ian, *Where Reincarnation and Biology Intersect:* detailed analysis of children who have physical marks and deformity form this life corresponding to past life wounds.

Tomlinson, *Healing the Eternal Soul:* emotions encountered in past life regression, detailed evidence and analysis of past-life regression research, chapter 1, the techniques used in interlife regression, chapter 7 and appendix III.

CHAPTER 1: TOWARDS THE LIGHT

Cannon, *Between Death and Life*: tunnel experience after death, chapter 1, pp. 12–13.

Fiore, *You Have Been Here Before*: tunnel experience after death, chapter 11, p. 223.

Lawton, *The Book of the Soul*: evidence against regression to non-human lives, chapter 7, pp. 194–5; detailed evidence and analysis of near-death experiences, chapter 2; severing of the cord, chapter 10, pp. 260–1.

Newton, *Journey of Souls*: tunnel experience after death, chapter 1, p.

9 and chapter 2, p. 18.

Modi, *Remarkable Healings*: tunnel experience after death, chapter 3, p. 144.

Ramster, *The Truth about Reincarnation*: tunnel experience after death, chapter 6, p. 133.

Tomlinson, *Healing the Eternal Soul*: additional case study of transition, chapter 7.

Van Lommel et al, *Near-death Experience in Survivors of Cardiac Arrest*; a prospective study in the Netherlands, The Lancet, 15 Dec 2001

Whitton, *Life Between Life*: tunnel experience after death, chapter 4, pp. 30–1.

CHAPTER 2: BECOMING WHOLE AGAIN

Cannon, *Between Death and Life*: initial healing, chapter 5, pp. 62–7; rest and recuperation for damaged souls, chapter 2, pp. 20.

Newton, *Journey of Souls*: initial healing, chapter 5, pp. 53–5; reorientation for mildly traumatized souls, chapter 5, pp. 55–6.

Modi, *Remarkable Healings*: initial healing, chapter 3, pp. 115–16; ventilation for traumatized souls, chapter 3, p. 115.

Newton, *Destiny of Souls*: reshaping or remodeling of traumatized souls, chapter 4, pp. 94–104; reintegrating soul energy, chapter 4, pp. 120–4.

Ramster, *The Truth About Reincarnation*: initial healing, chapter 6, pp. 133–4.

CHAPTER 3: REVIEWING OUR PAST LIVES

Lawton, *The Book of the Soul*: regression evidence against the notion of hell in Christian and Hindu theology, chapter 7, pp. 182–94.

Modi, *Remarkable Healings*: seeing past events from the perspective of others, chapter 3, p. 117.

Moody, *Life After Life*: life reviews during the near-death experiences, chapter 2, pp. 64-8

Newton, *Destiny of Souls*: soul perspective of feeling the pain inflicted on others, chapter 5, pp 167.

Ring, *Life at Death*: life review at the death experience, chapter 4, p67 and chapter 10, pp197-8

Tomlinson, *Healing the Eternal Soul*: additional case studies of guide review and of elder review, chapter 7.

Whitton, *Life Between Life*: seeing past events from the perspective of others, chapter 4, p. 40.

CHAPTER 4: WORKING WITH OUR SOUL GROUP

Lawton, *The Book of the Soul*: gender issues in the context of reincarnation, chapter 7, pp. 176–8.

Newton, *Journey of Souls*: dormant energy of still incarnate soul mates, chapter 6, p. 85; soul grading system by color, chapter 7, pp. 102–5; secondary groupings, chapter 7, pp. 87–91; one guide for each group, chapter 14, p. 262.

Tomlinson, *Healing the Eternal Soul*: additional case studies of soul groups, chapter 7.

CHAPTER 5: SPECIALIST ACTIVITIES

Lawton, *The Book of the Soul*: evidence in support of intelligent design, chapter 10, pp. 265–7.

Newton, *Destiny of Souls*: energy work, chapter 5, pp. 194–9 and chapter 8, pp. 330–44.

Newton, *Journey of Souls*: energy work, chapter 10, pp. 164–8.

Whitton, *Life Between Life*: halls of learning, chapter 4, p. 48.

CHAPTER 6: PLANNING OUR NEXT LIFE

Lawton, *The Seth Material* (paper at www.ianlawton.com/se1.htm).

Tomlinson, *Healing the Eternal Soul*: additional case studies of multiple choice previews, chapter 7.

CHAPTER 7: KARMIC DYNAMICS

Cannon, *Between Death and Life*: filler lives, chapter 8, p. 140.

Lawton, *The Book of the Soul*: detailed analysis of the dynamics of karma, chapter 7, pp. 154–70.

Newton, *Journey of Souls*: filler lives, chapter 12, p. 220.

CHAPTER 8: RETURNING TO INCARNATION

Newton, *Life Between Lives*: a soul drifting in and out until finally entering the brain of a fetus, Part 3, pp. 51

Newton, *Destiny of Souls*: proportion of soul energy brought into incarnation, chapter 4, pp. 116–20; difficult merger of soul and brain, chapter 9, pp. 384–94.

Tomlinson, *Healing the Eternal Soul*: additional case study of soul energy selection, embarkation and merger, chapter 7.

APPENDIX

Lawton, *The Book of the Soul*: analysis of interlife pioneers, chapter 5, pp. 122, chapter 6, pp 149.

BIBLIOGRAPHY

Cannon, Dolores, *Between Death and Life: Conversations With a Spirit*, Gateway, 2003.

Fiore, Edith, *You Have Been Here Before: A Psychologist Looks at Past Lives*, Ballantine Books, 1979.

Fiore, Edith, *The Unquiet Dead: A Psychologist Treats Spirit Possession*, Ballantine Books, 1988.

Lawton, Ian, *The Book of the Soul: Rational Spirituality for the Twenty-First Century*, Rational Spirituality Publishing, 2004.

Modi, Shakuntala, *Remarkable Healings: A Psychiatrist Uncovers Unsuspected Roots of Mental and Physical Illness*, Hampton Roads, 1997.

Modi, Shakuntala, *Memories of God and Creation: Remembering from the Subconscious Mind*, Hampton Roads, 2000.

Newton, Michael, *Destiny of Souls: New Case Studies of Life Between Lives*, Llewellyn, 2000

Newton, Michael, *Journey of Souls: Case Studies of Life Between Lives*, Llewellyn, 1994

Newton, Michael, *Life Between Lives: Hypnotherapy for Spiritual Regression*, Llewellyn, 2004.

Ramster, Peter, *The Truth about Reincarnation*, Rigby, 1980.

Ramster, Peter, *The Search for Lives Past*, Somerset Film & Publishing, 1992.

Stevenson, Ian, *Twenty Case of Suggested Reincarnation*, University Press of Vigina, 1974

Stevenson, Ian, *Where Reincarnation and Biology Intersect* (short version of two-volume *Reincarnation and Biology*), Praeger, 1997.

TenDam, Hans, *Exploring Reincarnation*, Rider, 2003.

Tomlinson, Andy, *Healing the Eternal Soul: Insights from Past Life and Spiritual Regression*, O Books, 2006.

Wambach, Helen, *Reliving Past Lives: The Evidence Under Hypnosis*, Hutchinson, 1979.

Wambach, Helen, *Life Before Life*, Bantam, 1979.

Weiss, Brian, *Many Lives, Many Masters*, Piatkus, 1994.

Whitton, Joel, and Fisher, Joe, *Life Between Life*, Warner Books, 1988.

Woolger, Roger, *Other Lives, Other Selves: A Jungian Psychotherapist Discovers Past Lives*, Bantam, 1988.

INDEX

Altruistic life 112, 114, 132-134, 169

Ancient wisdom 11

Astral realm 12-14, 169

Attachments 169

Cannon, Dolores 5, 27, 40, 132, 162

Core soul energy 48, 152, 169

Council 63, 69, 115-119, 169

Delayering 32-40, 44, 48, 144, 169

Earthbound soul 12

Elders; next life planning 114-120

Elders; past life review 63-71

Elders; role 5, 12, 36, 169

Emotional lessons 85, 89, 130-132, 169

Energy manipulation 93-96

Freewill 129-130

Karma 127-134, 170

Halls of learning 62, 89

Healing 27-40

Healing; trauma 40-44

Higher Ones 63, 169

Holographic soul 135,170

Hypnosis for interlife 6-7

Intellectual pursuits 89-93

Interlife; fluidity 53, 82, 158, 170

Interlife; history 161-162

Interlife; time 13, 144

Interlife; pioneer comparison 166-177

Interlife; research 163-165

Intuition 7, 87, 89, 136

Leaving the body 14-18

Library of life books 57-63, 68-71, 86-92, 123-124

Life path 111, 170

Life previews 101-125, 170

Light realm; definition 12-13, 170

Masters 63-4

Modi, Shakuntala 162

Near death; comparison with the interlife 22-25

Near death; experiences 11-12

Newton, Michael 4, 5, 8, 10, 23, 27, 40, 45, 48, 50, 78, 80, 82, 83, 93, 94, 105, 115, 121, 132, 135, 148, 157, 158, 162

Ramster, Peter 4, 23, 27, 161

Past life; death 11, 14-25

Past life; solitary review 51-53

Past life; spirit guide review 53-57

Past life; suicide review 60-63

Planning; elders 114-120

Planning; next life 97-125

Planning; single life options 101-105

Planning; multiple life options 105-114

Regression; definition 170

Relayering 143-147, 170

Rest in the spirit realm 44-45

Returning to incarnation 135-152

Soul; color 80, 171

Soul; energy split 135-143

Soul; energy reintegration 45-48, 171

Soul; experience 79-81

Soul; fragmentation 36-37, 171

Soul; level of development 80

Soul; level of vibration 12, 30, 34, 40, 44, 55, 148

Soul; merging with the body 147-151

Soul; perspective 50-51

Soul; perception 22, 25, 44

Soul; reshaping 40

Soul group; changing 83-84

Soul group; secondary 82, 123-124, 171

Soul group; theme 21, 64, 65, 71, 81, 82, 85, 92, 96, 130, 134

Soul group; planning 98-101

Soul group; primary 18, 73-84

Source; ultimate 60, 94, 171

Specialist activities 85-96

Specialist skills 130-132, 171

Spirit guide; definition 171

Spirit guide; influence 88-89

Spirit guide; meeting 13, 18-22, 33-36, 48-47

Spirit realms; definition 171

Spiritual regression 171

Subject feedback 154-159

Suicide 60-63, 98-99, 117-118, 136

Teachers 36, 85-89

Trapped soul energies 13, 16, 169, 172

Traumatic death 33, 38-39, 40-44

Triggers and reminders 121-125, 172

Veil of amnesia 151-152, 172

Wambach, Helen 4, 5, 161

Welcoming parties 18-23, 138

Whitton, Joel 4, 5, 50, 89, 161

Wise ones 63, 67, 120, 140, 172

THE AUTHOR

Andy Tomlinson is a psychology graduate and registered UK psychotherapist. He has been trained in Eriksonian hypnotherapy and regression therapy, and is an International Board of Regression Therapy certified past-life therapist. He is also a certified Life between Lives therapist with the Michael Newton Institute. Andy has run an internationally renowned private practice dedicated to regression therapy since 1996. He is currently the Director of Training for the Past Life Regression Academy, and a founder member of the European Academy of Regression Therapy. This is a group of European regression therapy organizations that work to the same quality standards. He is also one of the founding members of the European Association of Regression Therapy. Andy trains, lectures and gives talks internationally on past lives and the soul memories between them. His first book, *Healing the Eternal Soul*, was published in 2006. For further information about Andy or his training see his website: *www.regressionacademy.com*.

FURTHER READING

The Wisdom of the Soul - Ian Lawton, with research assistance from Andy Tomlinson, Rational Spirituality Press, 2007

In a startling experiment, ten groups of evolved spirits from the interlife share profound insights on such topics as: the purpose of life on earth; the future of humanity; and the true nature of time and reality. This is an amazing book to read and it provides valuable information on a range of spiritual, historical and philosophical topics.

Healing the Eternal Soul - Andy Tomlinson, O Books, 2006

Within each of us reside memories of past lives. Many are traumatic memories that are re-created making little sense in the context of our present life. This practical manual covers the theory and techniques needed to heal them and includes regression into the interlife. It is recommended for both the spiritually aware reader and any healer.

Journey of Souls - Michael Newton, Llewellyn, 1994

Further graphic detail is provided of what it feels like to die and cross over, who meets us, where we go, and what we do in the spirit realms before choosing the next body for incarnation. The narrative is based on the interlife accounts of twenty-nine people. This important book provides another foundation for mapping out the interlife experience.

O books

O is a symbol of the world, of oneness and unity. In different cultures it also means the "eye", symbolizing knowledge and insight, and in Old English it means "place of love or home". O books explores the many paths of understanding which different traditions have developed down the ages, particularly those today that express respect for the planet and all of life. In philosophy, metaphysics and aesthetics O as zero relates to infinity, indivisibility and fate. In Zero Books we are developing a list of provocative shorter titles that cross different specializations and challenge conventional academic or majority opinion.

For more information on the full list of over 300 titles please visit our website
www.O-books.net

myspiritradio is an exciting web, internet, podcast and mobile phone global broadcast network for all those interested in teaching and learning in the fields of body, mind, spirit and self development. Listeners can hear the show online via computer or mobile phone, and even download their favourite shows to listen to on MP3 players whilst driving, working, or relaxing.

Feed your mind, change your life with O Books,
The O Books radio programme carries interviews with most authors, sharing their wisdom on life, the universe and everything...e mail questions and co-create the show with O Books and myspiritradio.

Just visit **www.myspiritradio.com** for more information.